THE JAPANESE HOME STYLEBOOK

THE JAPANESE

HOME STYLEBOOK

Architectural Details and Motifs

Illustrations by
Saburo Yamagata

Edited by
Peter Goodman

Stone Bridge Press
Berkeley, California

Published by STONE BRIDGE PRESS
P.O. Box 8208, Berkeley, CA 94707

Adapted from *Shinpan Washitsu
Zosaku Shusei* by Saburo Yamagata.
© 1979 Saburo Yamagata.
Original Japanese edition published
by K.K. Gakugei Shuppan-Sha in 1979.
English adaptation rights arranged by
K.K. Gakugei Shuppan-Sha through
Japan Foreign Rights Centre.

English text © 1992 Stone Bridge Press.

First English-language edition, 1992.

10 9 8 7 6 5 4 3 2

Printed in the United States of America.

Book design by Stephanie Young.
Composition by Harrington-Young,
Albany, CA.

LIBRARY OF CONGRESS
CATALOGING-IN-PUBLICATION DATA
Yamagata, Saburo.
    [Shinpan washitsu zosaku shusei. English]
    The Japanese home stylebook :
architectural details and motifs / illustrations
by Saburo Yamagata; edited by Peter
Goodman.—1st English-language ed.
        p.   cm.
    ISBN 1-880656-01-9
    1. Architecture—Japan—Details.
2. Vernacular architecture—Japan.
I. Goodman, Peter. II. Title.
NA1550.Y35513   1992
728'.37'0952—dc20   92-32075
                                    CIP

CONTENTS

The Japanese Home Stylebook contains drawings of some 1,800 different designs used in traditional Japanese residential architecture. Included are designs for windows, sliding *shoji* and *fusuma* screens, doors, decorative alcoves (*tokonoma*), transoms, ceilings, shelves, *tatami* mat arrangements, verandas, railings, and garden fences and paths. The book concludes with decorative motifs based on lattices and family crests.

So many patterns in so many variations may seem at odds with the Western notion that the classical Japanese home is "simple" or "spare" or "modest." But we mistake a lack of furniture—a Japanese room may have only a low table, some cushions, and a small cabinet—for a lack of flair. This is because we're looking at the space *within* the room. Our attention should instead be focused on the flat surfaces that *surround* the room, at the walls, the floor, and the ceiling. Here we will find a vigorous design sensibility at work. This sensibility gives pleasure to the observing eye. More important, it manipulates light and articulates lines of sight so they penetrate and commingle within the room in particular ways. The internal density of the room is in fact fashioned from these surface designs along the room's perimeters. A human being in the confluence of such design energies—if the design is skilled—floats satisfied in the fullness of space.

Look at these surfaces in turn.

Floors.   The Japanese-style floor is for kneeling or sleeping. As the only room surface with a tactile role, it directly connects the inhabitant to the room. The floor is laid out in units of woven straw tatami mats, each mat being roughly the size of a human being. All the modular elements in the Japanese room derive their scale from this fundamental unit of measure.

Ceilings.   Japanese ceilings use surface decoration, texturing, and slope (pitch) to modify and subdivide the volume of the room, thus framing the human activity on the floor. In some of the drawings in this book, you can see that even within a single small room there can be several different ceiling designs.

6

Walls.   Because the Japanese home is of post-and-beam construction, its walls are free to serve nonstructural purposes. Many "walls" in a Japanese home are actually lightweight sliding panels of striking design that, as they move, alter the light and change the volume of the room. Windows and transoms also control lighting, but just as importantly use two-dimensional horizontal and vertical elements (wooden and bamboo lattices) to affect how the three-dimensional volumes of the room are perceived by the room's inhabitant.

The important role human perception plays in the spatial design of the Japanese room is suggested by American landscape designer David A. Slawson in his book *Secret Teachings in the Art of Japanese Gardens.* Slawson discusses how "sensory values" and "cultural values" in Japanese garden design help persuade the observer of the garden to participate in the creation of the garden aesthetic. Sensory values involve texture, perspective, layering, and coloring techniques that convince the eye to see, for example, a broad vista in what is but a small corner of a backyard. Cultural values are evoked by designs with religious or historical significance—a "turtle-shaped" garden mound as a symbol of longevity would be an example.

One can see both types of values at work in the architectural details reproduced in this book. Vertical and horizontal shapes predominate for obvious structural reasons, but notice how tension is added by the asymmetrical staggered-shelf design next to the *tokonoma* alcove, and how important light and shadow control is to the creation of depth. Notice too the many representational designs suggesting seasons, places, plants, and animals with very specific connotations for Japanese observers. Slawson would argue that an American homeowner looking for a "pure" Japanese treatment on a transom design should seriously consider, in place of cherry blossoms and insects, a bucking bronco and a cactus. The point, of course, is that the designs you choose must be true to their setting and resonate as they work together—but they must also make "sense" to you.

7

The designs in this book come mostly from what are called *shoin*-style buildings. An evolved form of this style called *sukiya shoin* borrowed many elements from the gentrified peasant aesthetic of the tea ceremony. These styles became fully developed in the 16th and 17th centuries and since then have defined what most people—in Japan and abroad—consider classical Japanese architectural elegance. The centerpiece of the home is the room with the tokonoma, and it is here that most of the design elements shown in this book can be found. The tokonoma room was where guests were entertained and was thus where the homeowner would show off his good taste and his ability to afford the finest craftsmanship. Tea taste is especially evident in the use of natural materials like reeds in the doors, as well as in the decorated ceilings and garden fences. Some of the designs are frankly quite audacious.

The late architect Saburo Yamagata, author and illustrator of the original Japanese version of this book, provided with his drawings many technical details for architects and woodworkers. These have been left out of this English-language edition, which is designed as a visual compendium of patterns and motifs. On page 176, however, is a list of books that do discuss Japanese carpentry and building techniques, as well as books of photographs that show complete rooms with all the design elements in place.

In the foreword to his book Mr. Yamagata, in typically modest Japanese fashion, apologizes for any inadequacies in his drawings, all of which he produced himself by hand. Any Westerner holding this book will surely agree that no apology is necessary. Doubtless many of the old buildings housing the details that Mr. Yamagata based his drawings on have been destroyed to make way for new roads and apartment complexes. Without his efforts, these wonderful designs might have been lost forever. Thanks to those efforts, they will endure and even, perhaps, take up residence abroad.

—P.G.

TOKONOMA AND SHELVES

The tokonoma is an alcove along one wall of a Japanese-style room. Next to it is often a companion alcove with asymmetrical staggered-shelf and cabinet arrangements. The floor of the tokonoma is usually several inches off the floor to set off a flower arrangement, vase, or hanging scroll that can be changed to fit the occasion and the season. In the corner on the adjacent wall may be a bench-like desk for writing, and above that a window, shoji screen, or transom to admit light into the room. Between the tokonoma and the shelf nook is a shaved post, prized for its dramatic shape. The shelf and cabinet arrangements are a marvel of visual complexity that play against the more stable horizontal and vertical spaces of the room.

Tokonoma

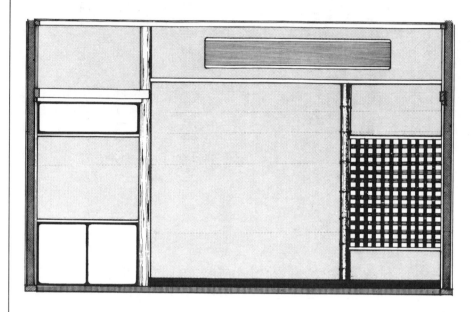

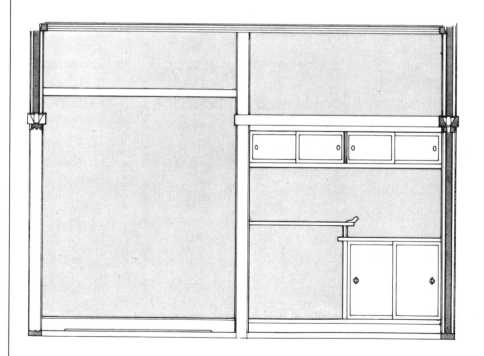

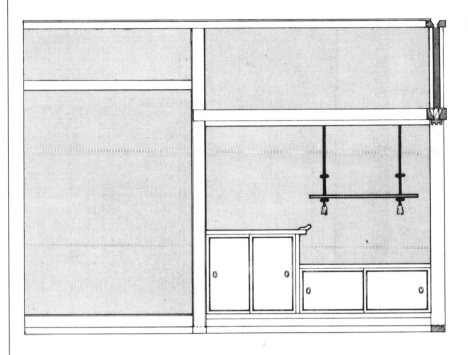

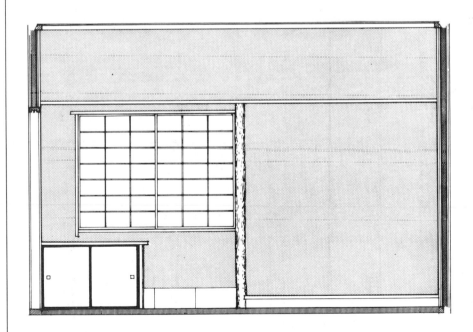

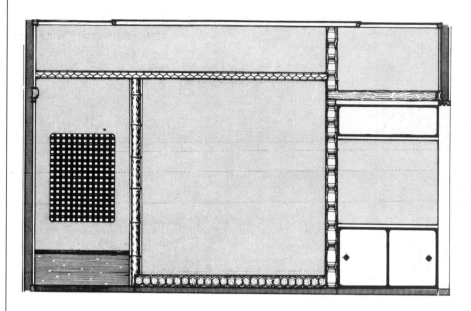

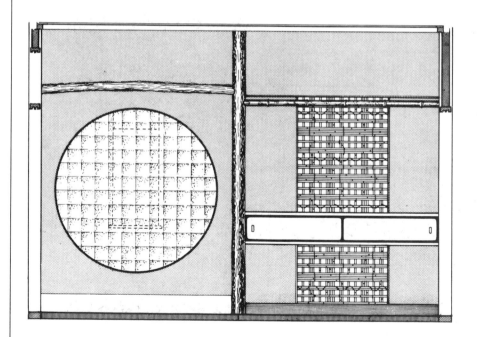

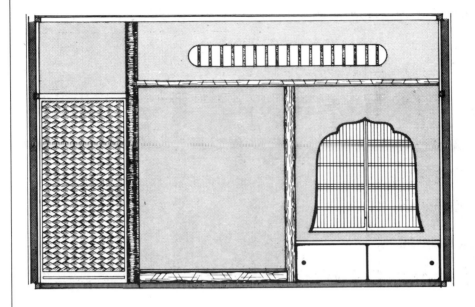

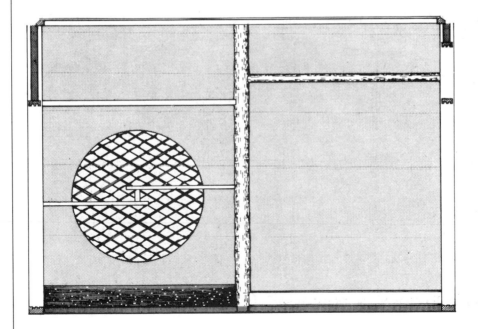

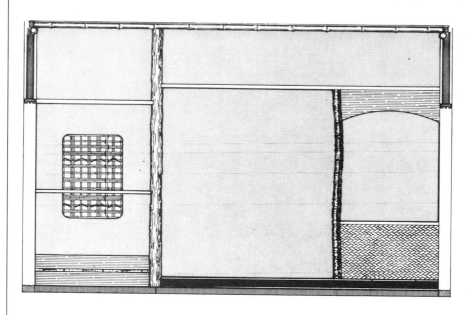

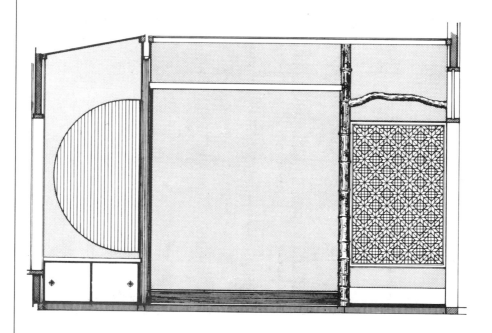

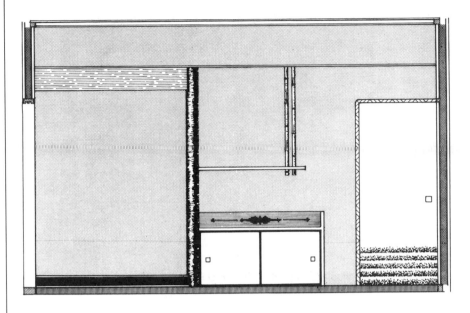

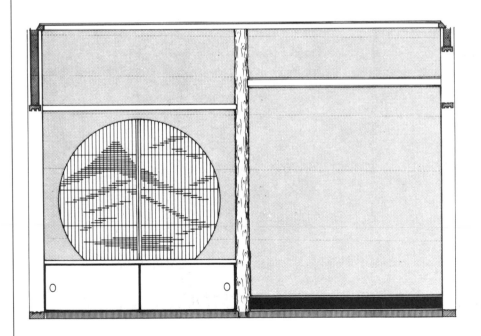

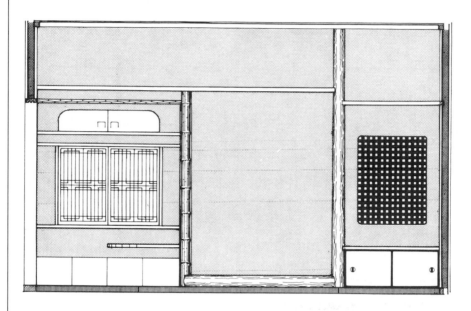

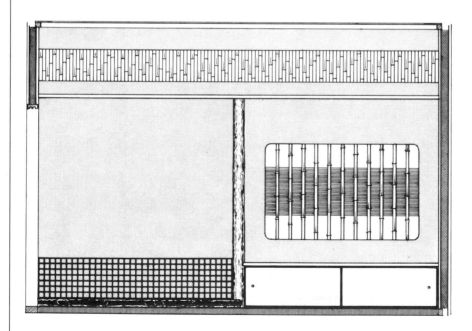

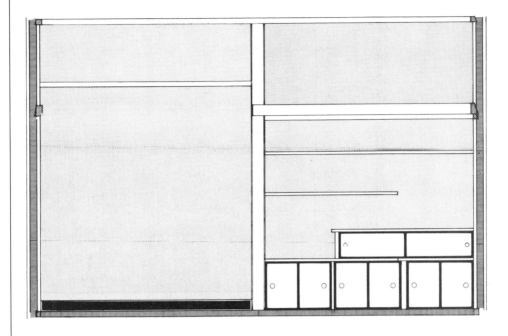

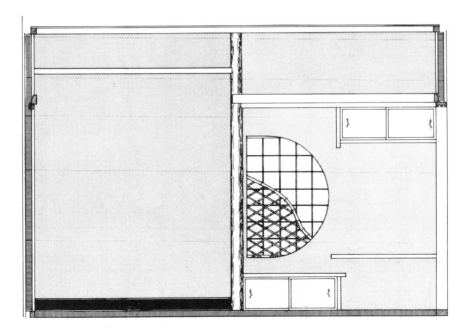

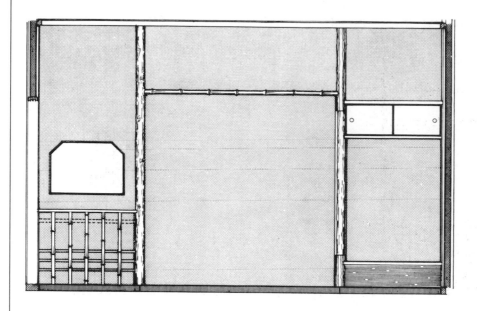

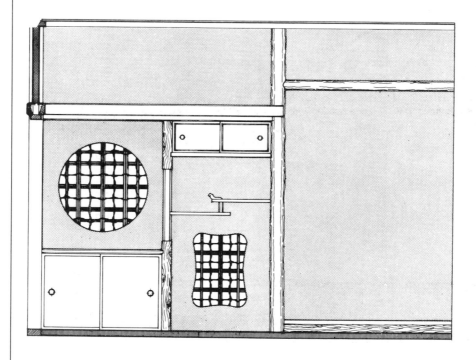

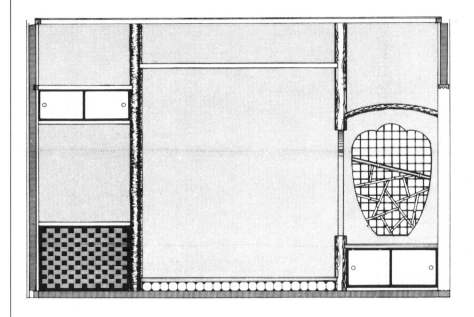

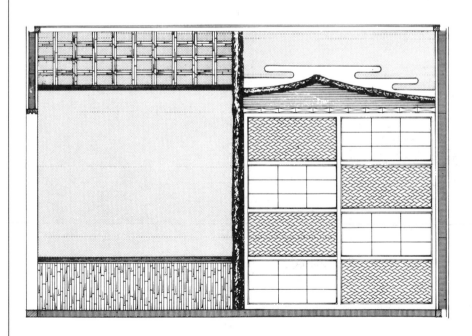

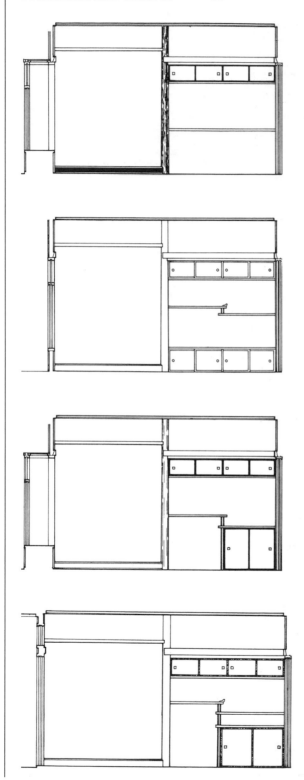

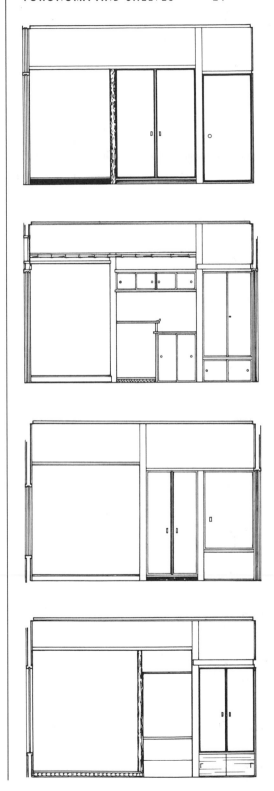

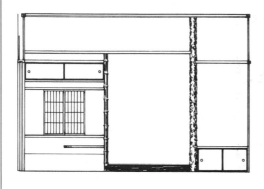

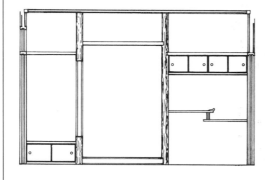

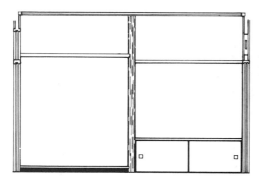

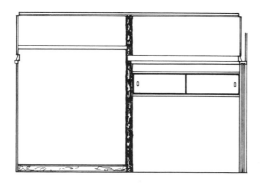

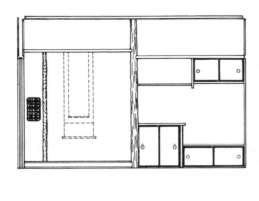

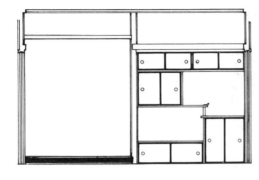

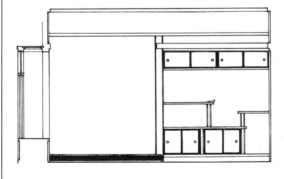

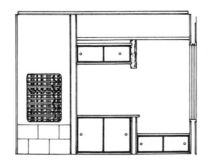

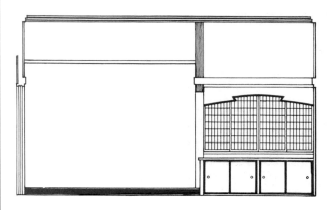

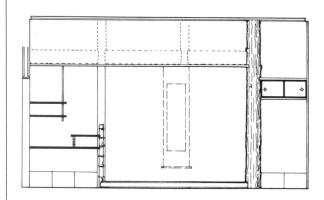

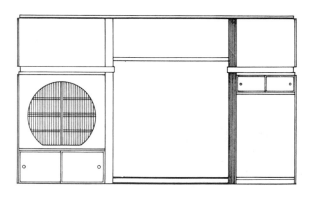

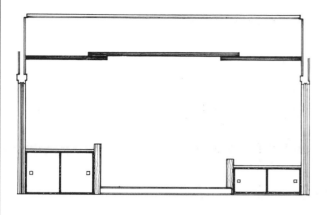

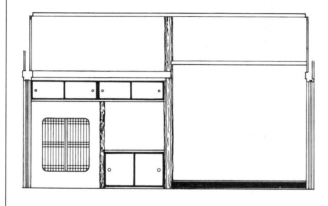

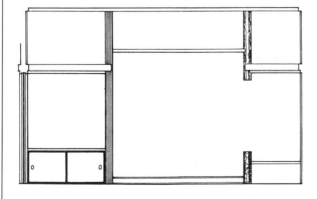

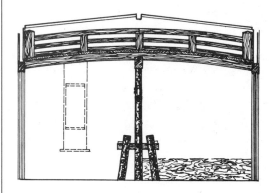

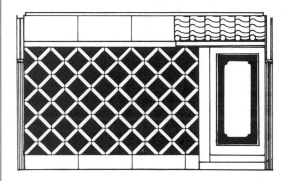

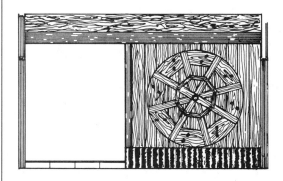

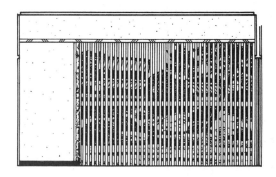

Traditional Staggered Shelf Arrangements

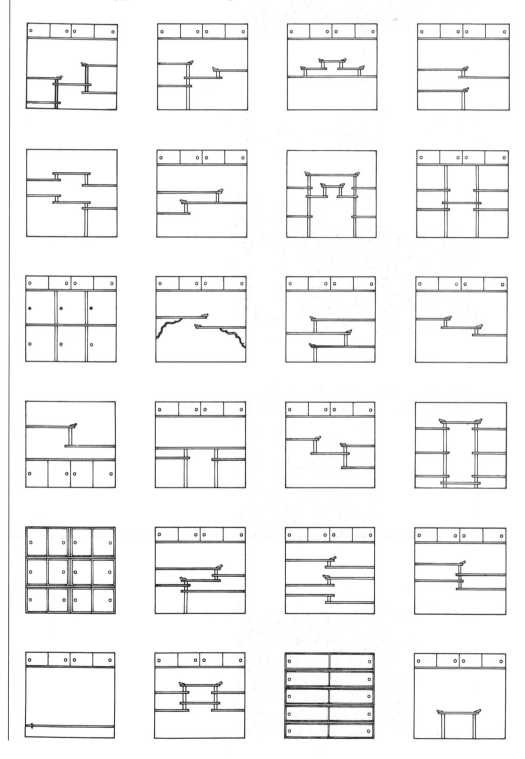

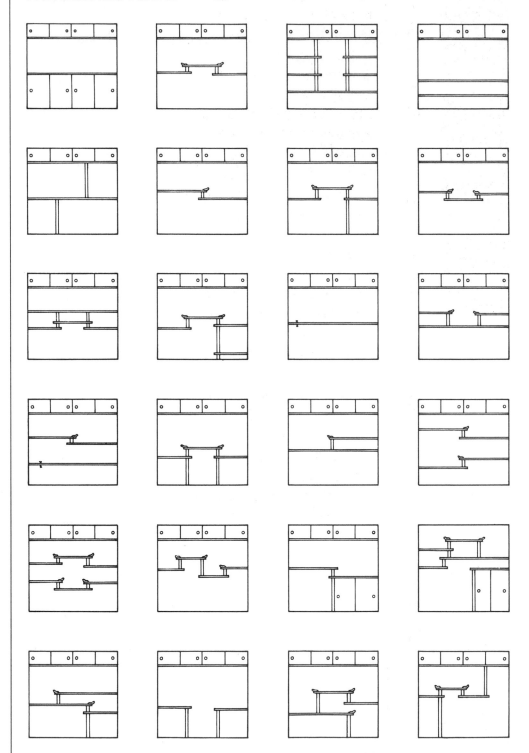

T A T A M I   M A T S   A N D   C E I L I N G S

Tatami mats are about 6 feet x 3 feet x 2 inches in size. Made of reed and straw, and bordered with cloth, they are used for sitting or sleeping on. Shoes and even slippers are never worn on tatami, so a tatami room encourages soft footfalls and gentle movement. In a tatami room, because you are generally seated or kneeling, eye level is down toward the floor. A playful designer will exploit this lowered field of vision by positioning objects so they become visible only after you are settled in the room. The decorated ceiling can also be more easily admired when you are seated. Ceilings over different parts of the room may have different textures and pitches (6–7 feet) to "frame" the activity taking place below. Many of the ceilings shown here are from tearooms—some are quite ornate, despite the generally austere ideals of the tea aesthetic.

Tatami Mat Arrangements

Tatami mats define one of the essential modular units in Japanese home construction. To this day, room sizes are indicated by the number of mats they contain (although the modern mat—and thus the modern room based on it—is smaller than it was in the past). How the mats are laid out on the floor is important; some arrangements are traditionally considered propitious and others are associated with funerals. In the drawings here, the "unlucky" arrangements are indicated by a diamond (♦).

3-mat designs   4.5-mat designs   winter tea   summer tea

6-mat designs   8-mat designs

10-mat designs

12-mat designs

14-mat designs

18-mat designs

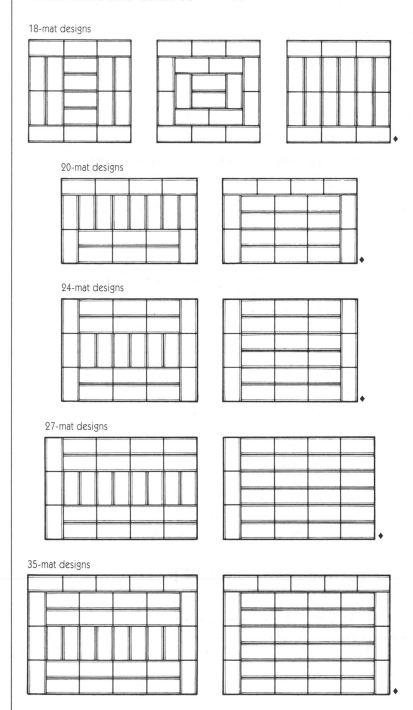

20-mat designs

24-mat designs

27-mat designs

35-mat designs

Sukiya Ceilings (flat and pitched)

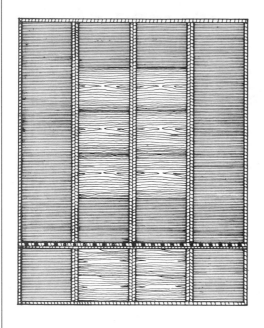

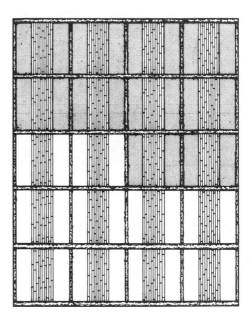

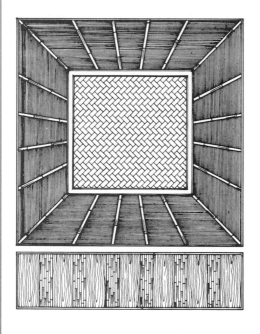

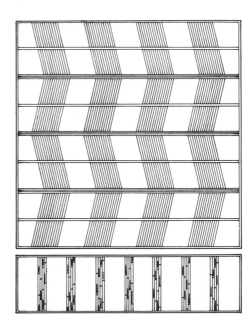

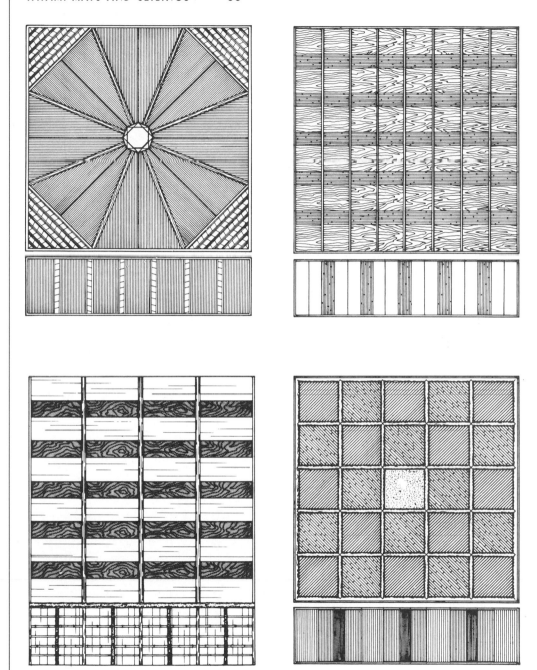

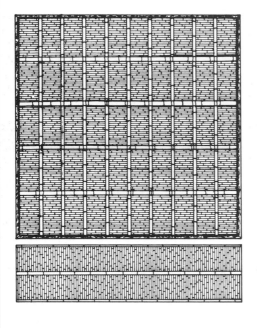

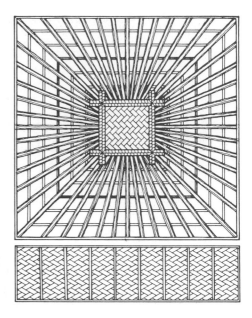

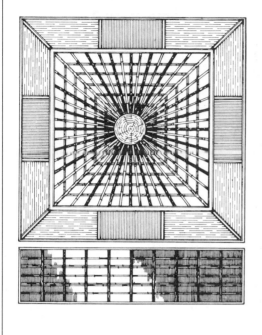

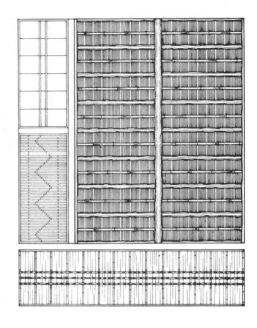

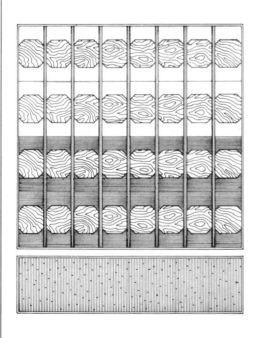

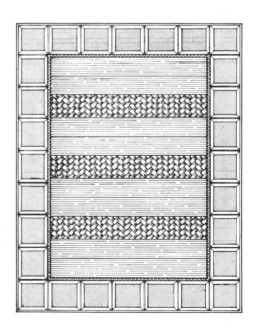

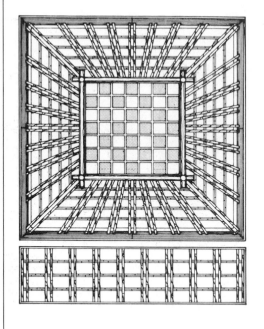

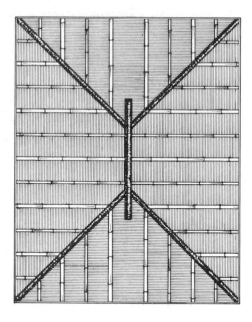

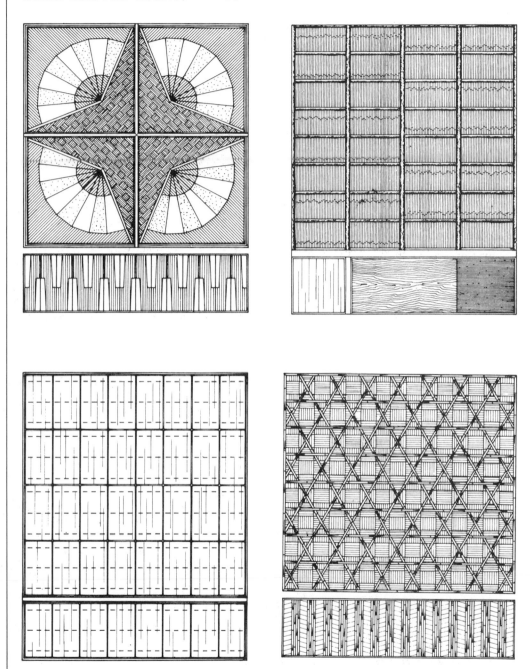

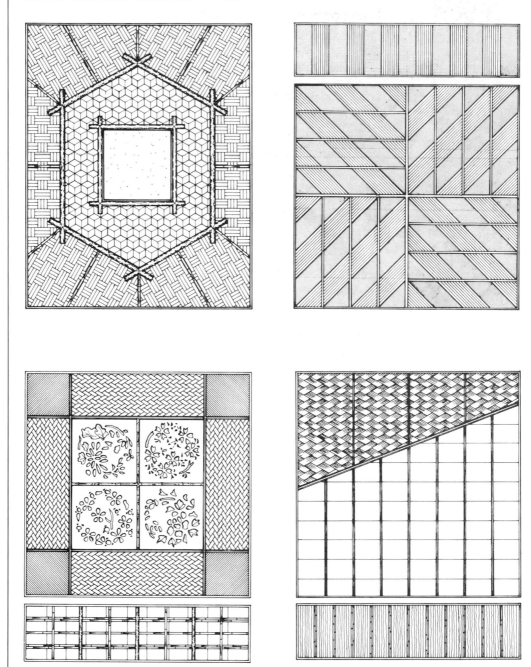

T R A N S O M S

Transoms (*ranma*) are used in the approximately 1–2 foot space between the ceiling and the horizontal lintel beam along the wall. They have the very practical function of admitting light and controlling ventilation when the fusuma or shoji that run below the lintel are closed (some Japanese rooms can be entirely surrounded by other rooms with no external wall into which a window can be opened). Transoms are viewed from both sides, so the quality of light in the room beyond is important to set off the design. Transoms make evident all the versatility and skill of the Japanese craftsman; they can be highly decorative and fanciful as well as plain and geometric. Typical constructions include carved openwork, bamboo trellises, and open or paper-covered (shoji-style) lattices.

Geometrical Designs

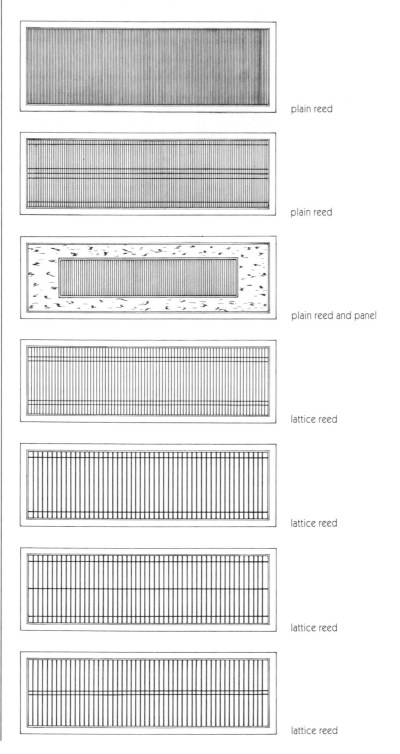

plain reed

plain reed

plain reed and panel

lattice reed

lattice reed

lattice reed

lattice reed

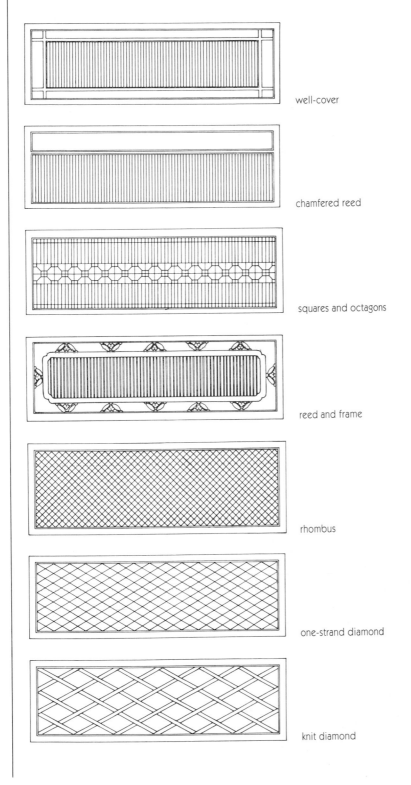

well-cover

chamfered reed

squares and octagons

reed and frame

rhombus

one-strand diamond

knit diamond

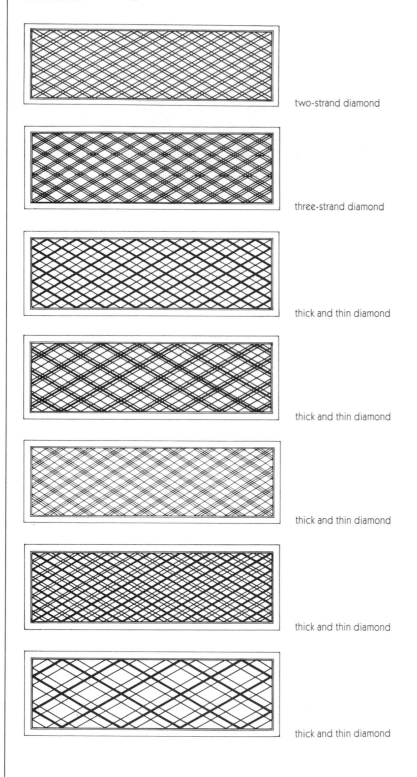

two-strand diamond

three-strand diamond

thick and thin diamond

thick and thin diamond

thick and thin diamond

thick and thin diamond

thick and thin diamond

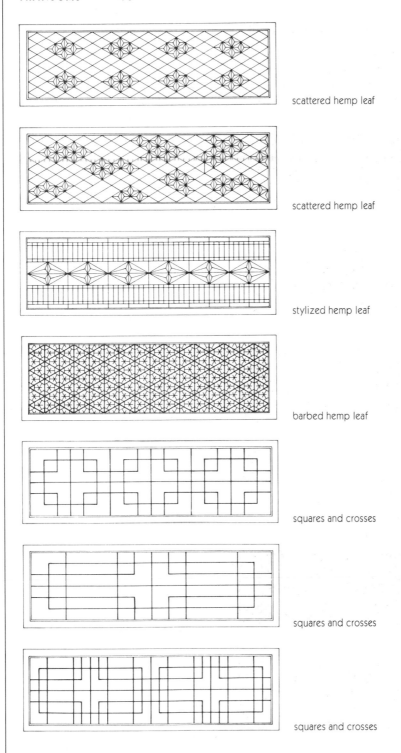

scattered hemp leaf

scattered hemp leaf

stylized hemp leaf

barbed hemp leaf

squares and crosses

squares and crosses

squares and crosses

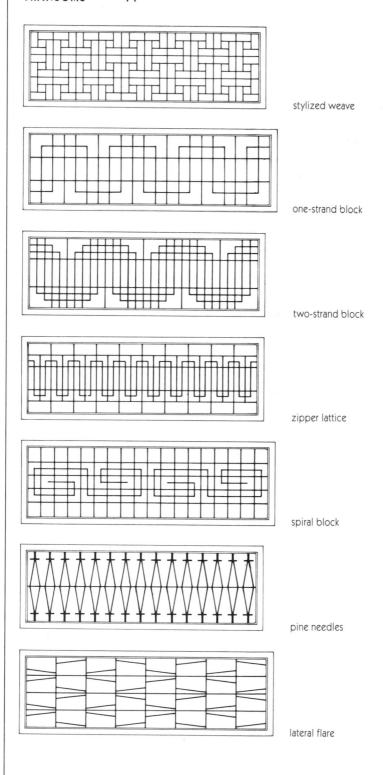

stylized weave

one-strand block

two-strand block

zipper lattice

spiral block

pine needles

lateral flare

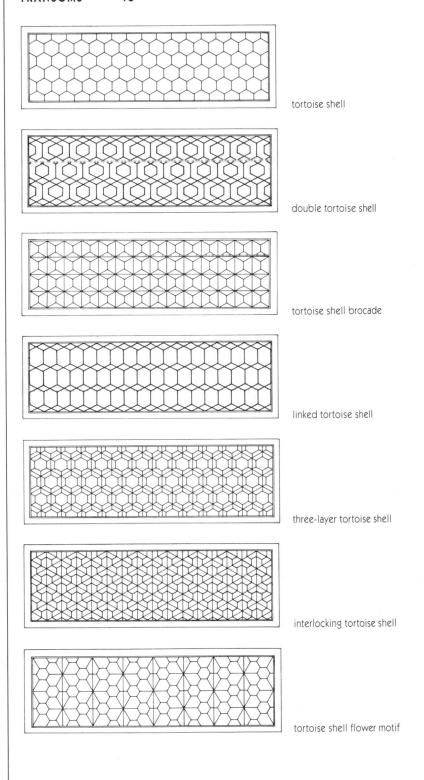

tortoise shell

double tortoise shell

tortoise shell brocade

linked tortoise shell

three-layer tortoise shell

interlocking tortoise shell

tortoise shell flower motif

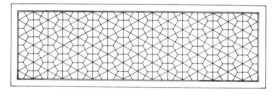

large interlocking tortoise shell

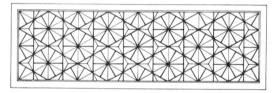

pointed tortoise shell

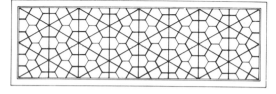

interlocking tortoise shell

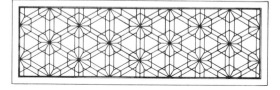

interlocking tortoise shell

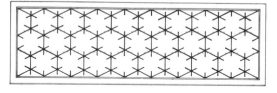

snowflake tortoise shell

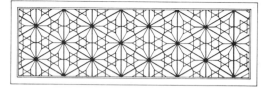

snowflake tortoise shell

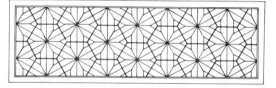

tortoise shell Chinese bellflower

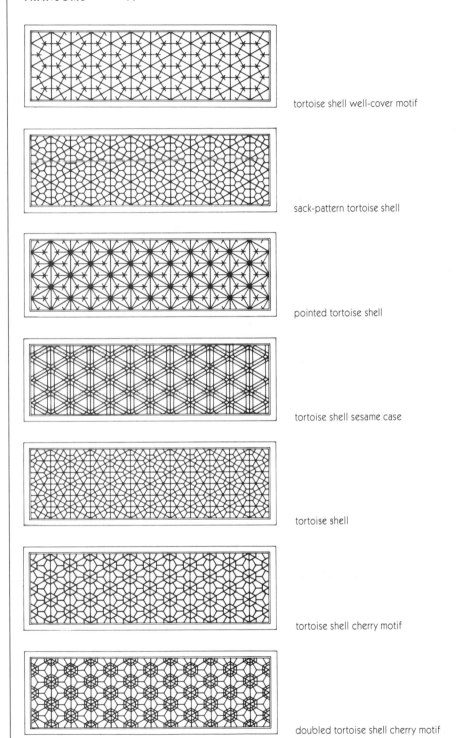

tortoise shell well-cover motif

sack-pattern tortoise shell

pointed tortoise shell

tortoise shell sesame case

tortoise shell

tortoise shell cherry motif

doubled tortoise shell cherry motif

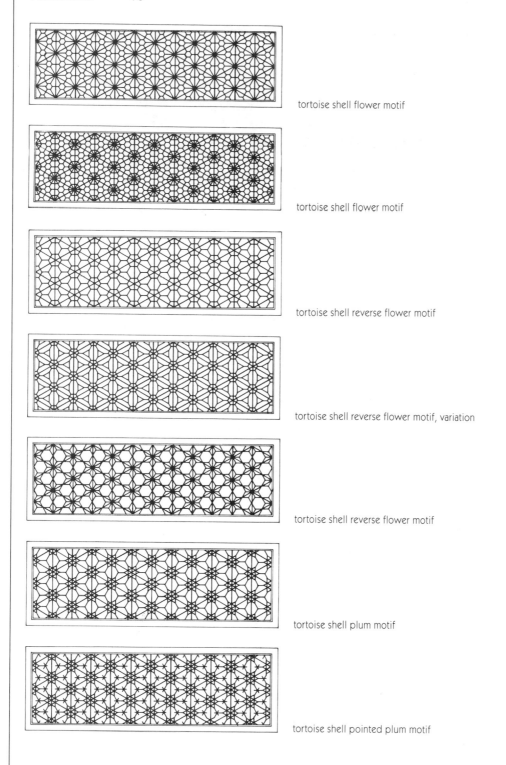

tortoise shell flower motif

tortoise shell flower motif

tortoise shell reverse flower motif

tortoise shell reverse flower motif, variation

tortoise shell reverse flower motif

tortoise shell plum motif

tortoise shell pointed plum motif

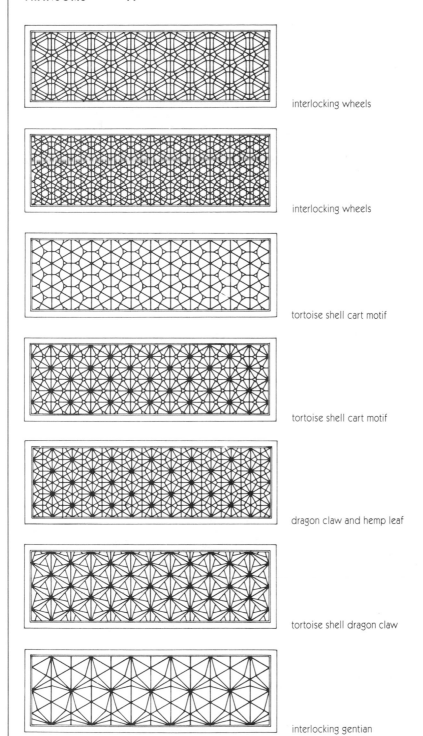

interlocking wheels

interlocking wheels

tortoise shell cart motif

tortoise shell cart motif

dragon claw and hemp leaf

tortoise shell dragon claw

interlocking gentian

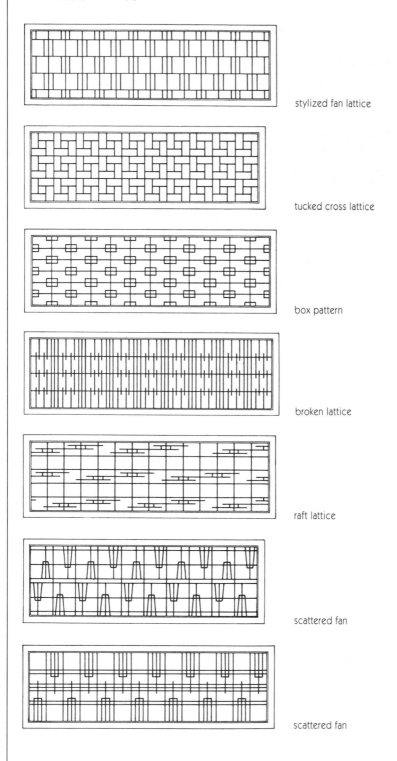

stylized fan lattice

tucked cross lattice

box pattern

broken lattice

raft lattice

scattered fan

scattered fan

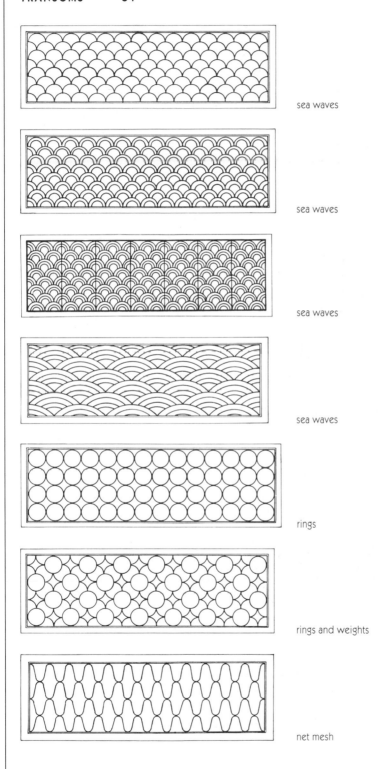

sea waves

sea waves

sea waves

sea waves

rings

rings and weights

net mesh

Openwork Designs

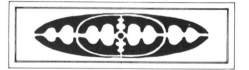 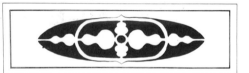

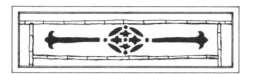

Representational Designs

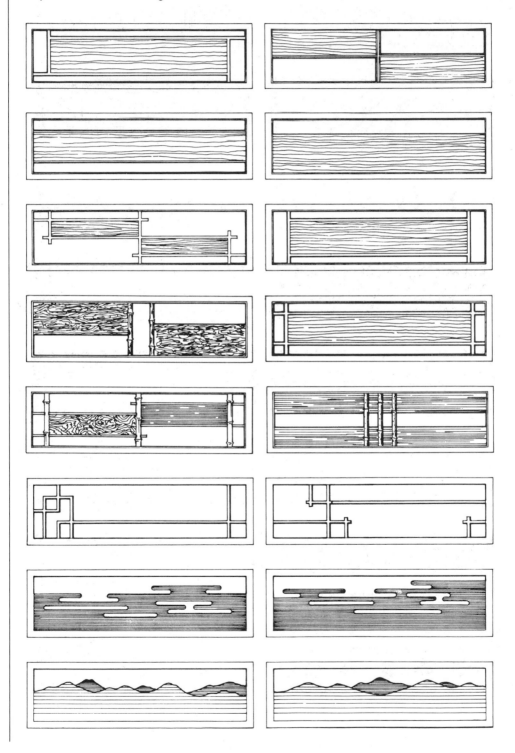

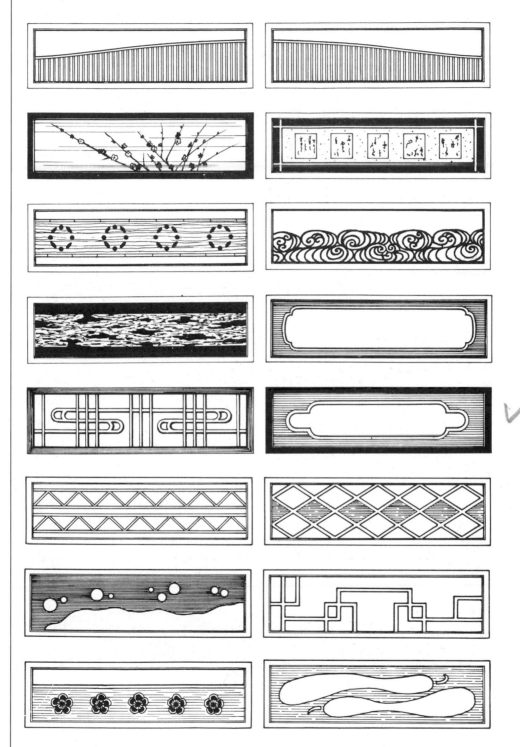

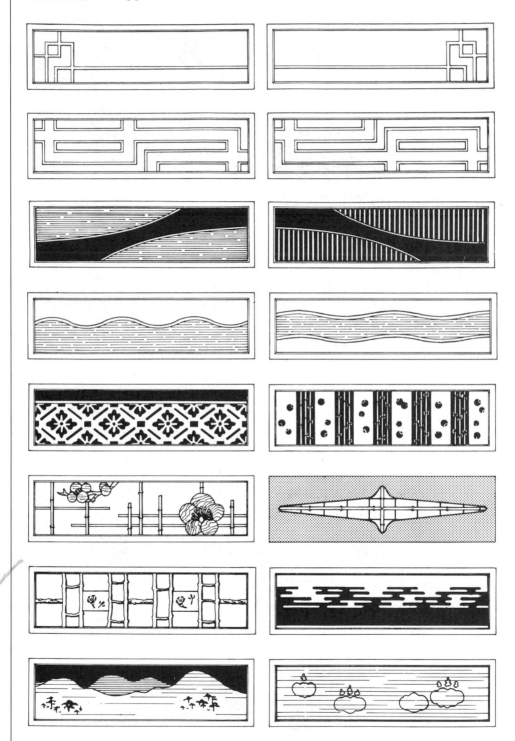

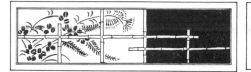

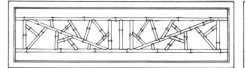

F U S U M A

Fusuma are lightweight fabric-covered doors—about the size of tatami mats—that fit between the lintel beam and the floor. Set in parallel tracks, fusuma can slide behind each other, or they can be lifted out and removed. Functionally, fusuma allow you to open and close off rooms as you please, sectioning off a large banquet hall, for example, into smaller, more intimate areas and vice versa. They thus exemplify the tremendous flexibility offered by Japanese modular design. As broad flat expanses, fusuma lend themselves to surface decoration and even freehand painting. Fusuma constructions are also used for closet and cabinet doors. Unlike shoji, fusuma do not admit light. Designs in metal, wood, ceramic, and even leather can be used for the *hikite,* or screen pulls.

Fusuma Designs

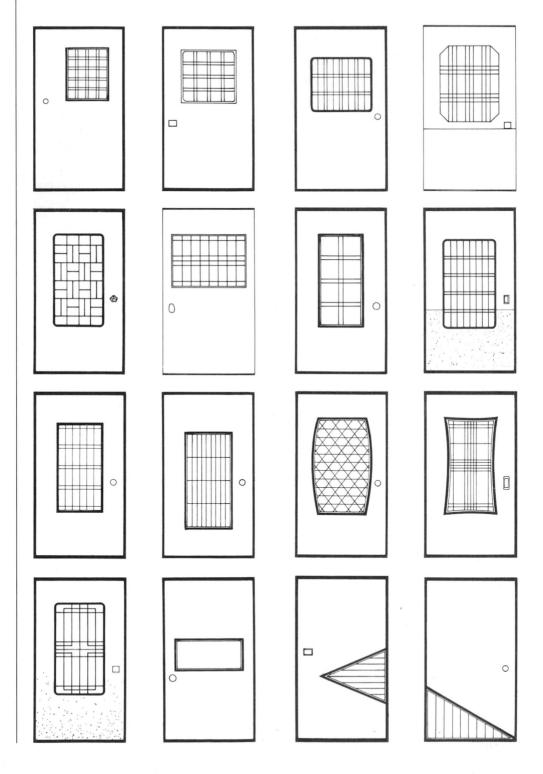

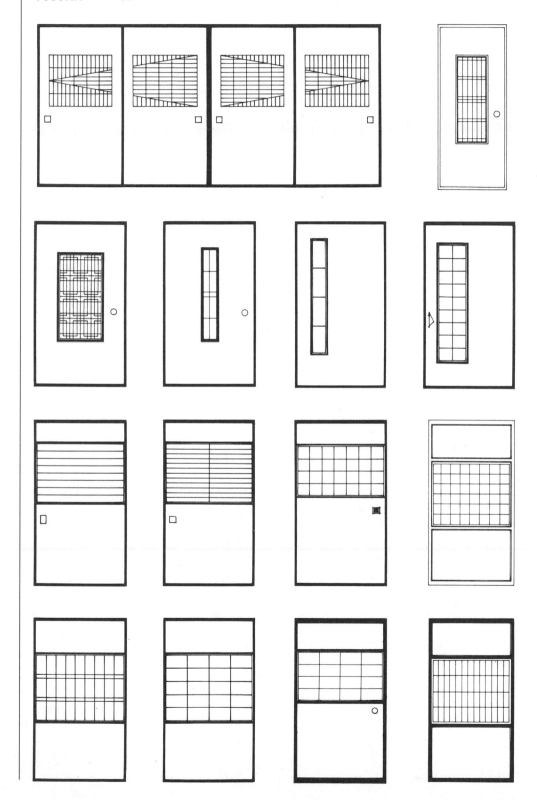

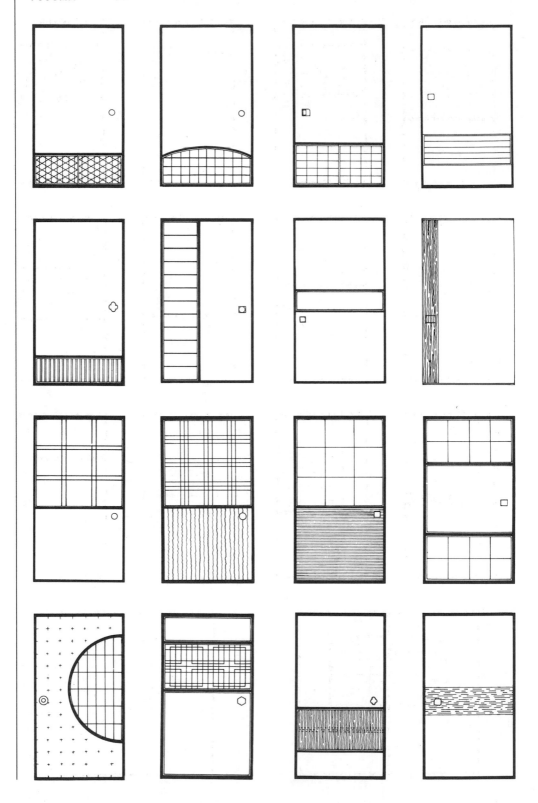

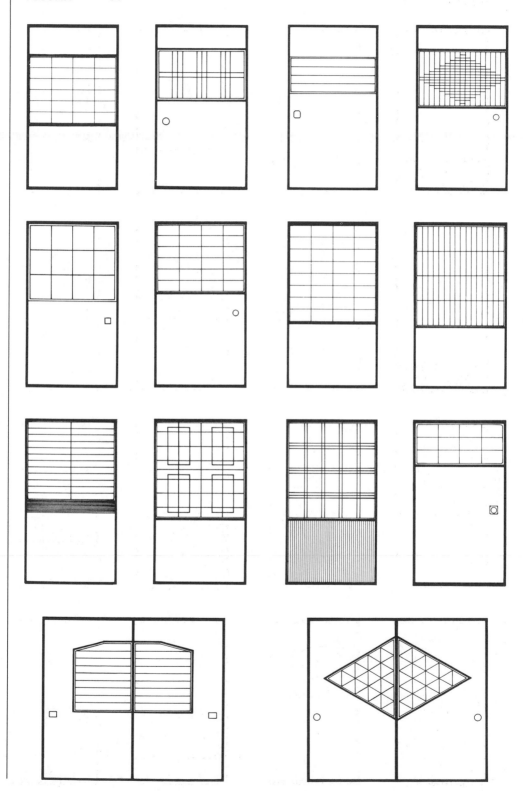

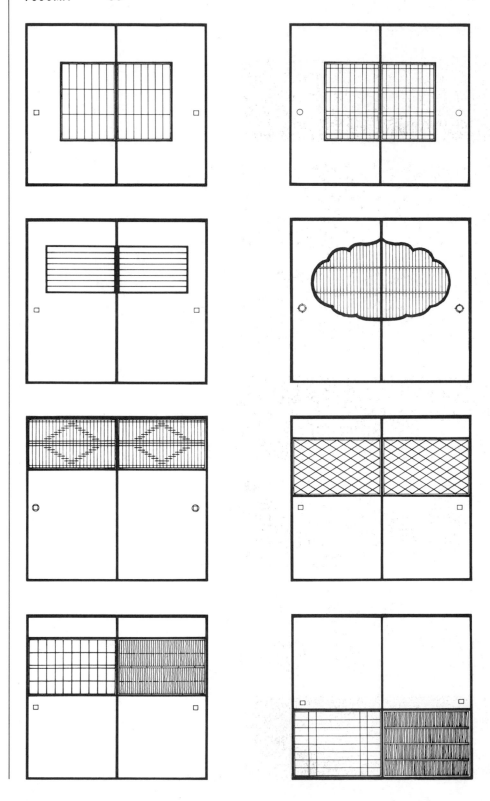

Fusuma Paper Patterns

pine

twill

waves

paulownia flower

Japanese maple

larch

pampas grass

chrysanthemum arabesque

grass clumps

foil-cut paulownia

gnarled-bark cloud

"Genji" cloud

autumn grasses

paulownia flowers

sea waves

cherry arabesque

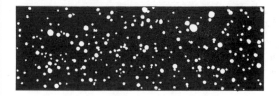

twill

hailstones

flowers and circles

pine, bamboo, and plum

sea waves

small paulownia flowers

bowls

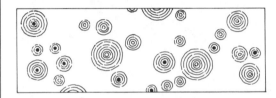

spirals

pine arabesque

swirling stream

pine and plum wheels

bamboo grass

Fusuma Pull Handles

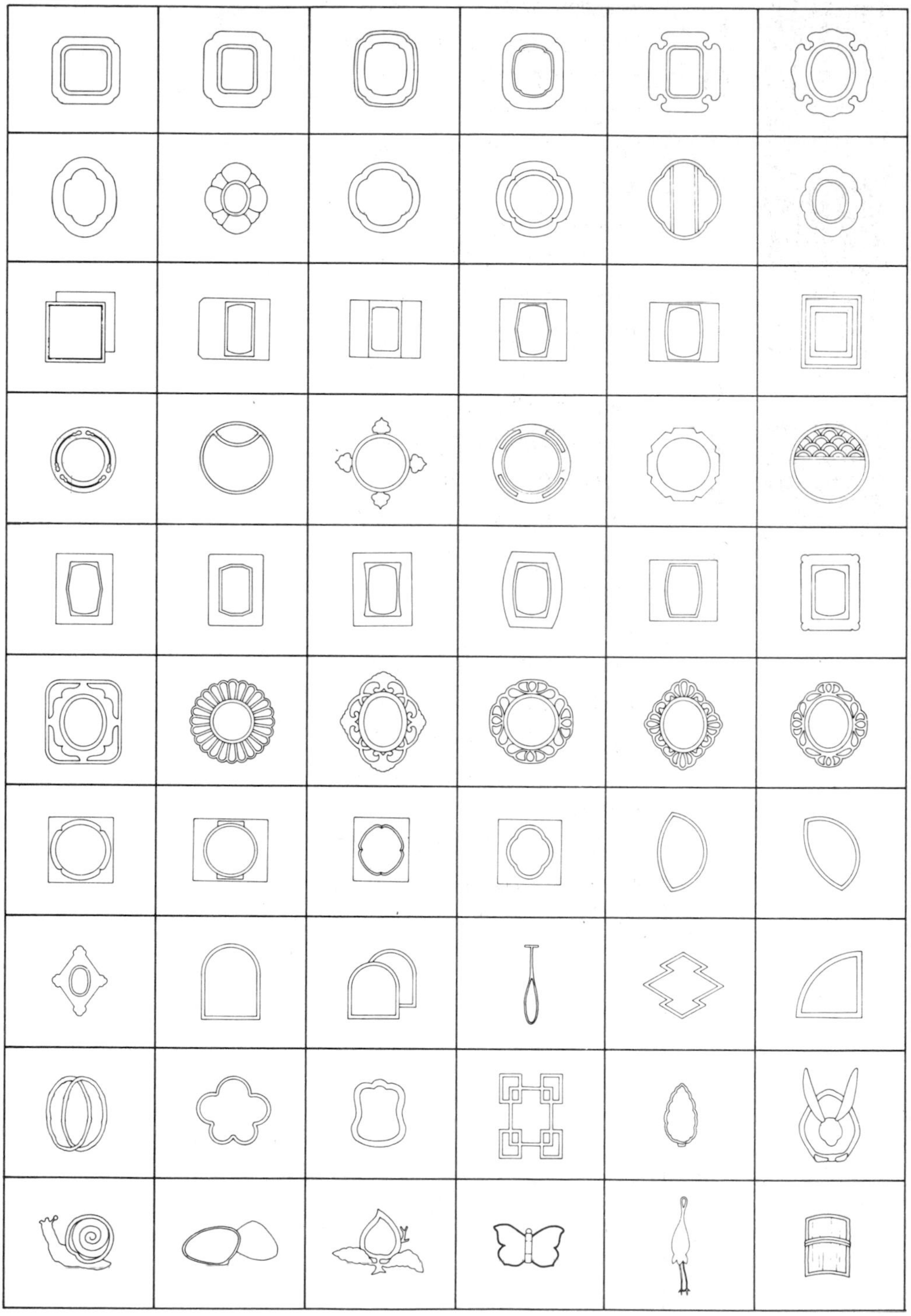

SHOJI SCREENS

Shoji screens consist of a wooden lattice with a white paper backing. The screens are placed between a room and the outside veranda and, like fusuma, they slide in tracks. When open they can frame a view and bring the external garden directly into the interior of the home. Most shoji in Japan are single sided, but double-framed shoji have been widely adopted in the West. Shoji fitted with protective hipboards at the base are best in high-traffic areas. Shoji treatments are also given to windows, cabinet doors, and transoms. The power of shoji comes from its graphic value as well as its ability to transmit light. Seemingly two dimensional, shoji design insinuates itself into every corner of the Japanese room, creating a shadowy, filtered, and voluminous world that many critics have seen as psychologically comforting, even mystical.

Shoin-style Shoji

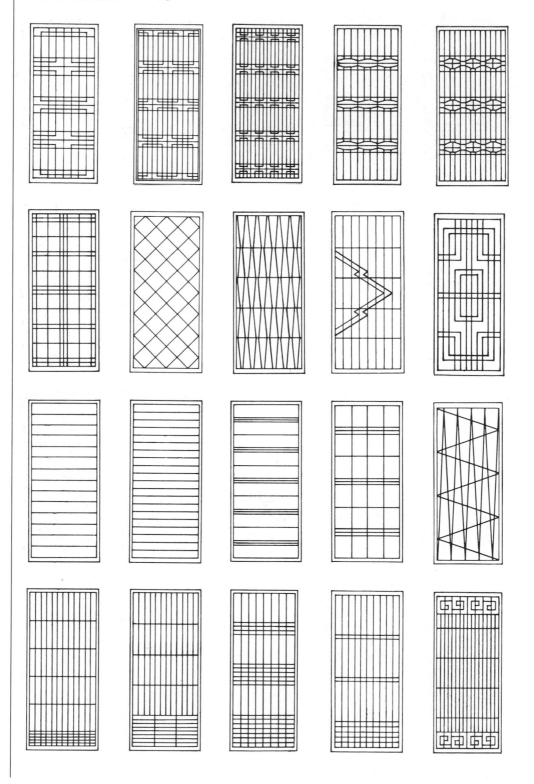

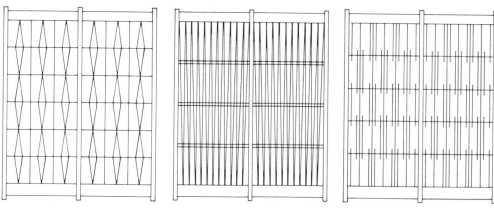

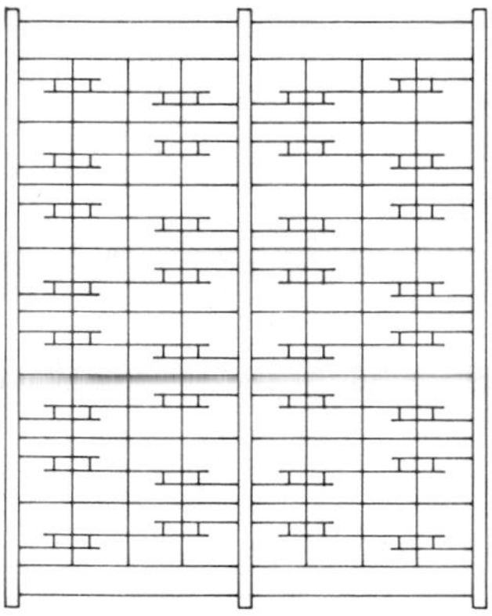
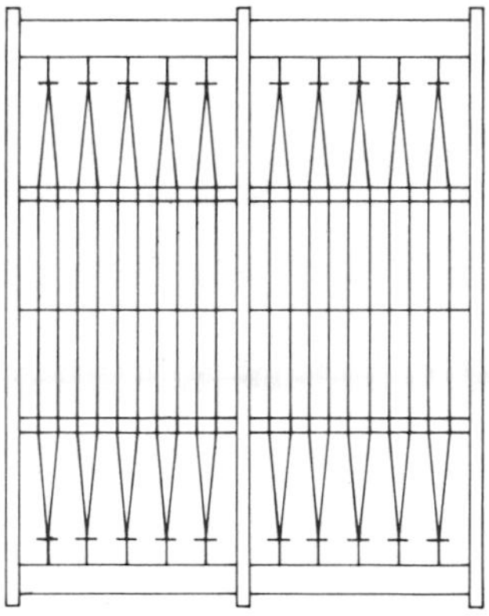
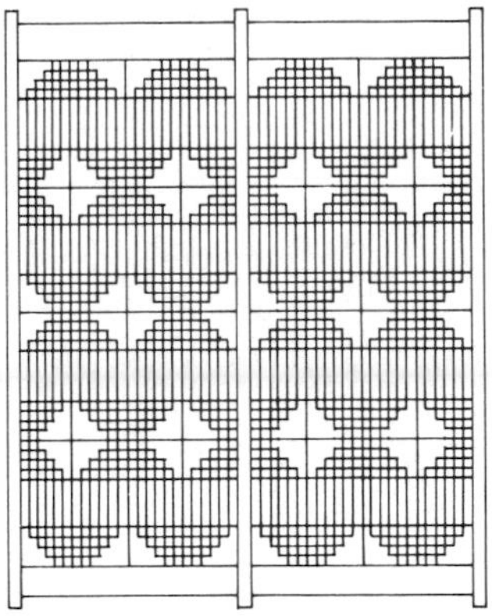
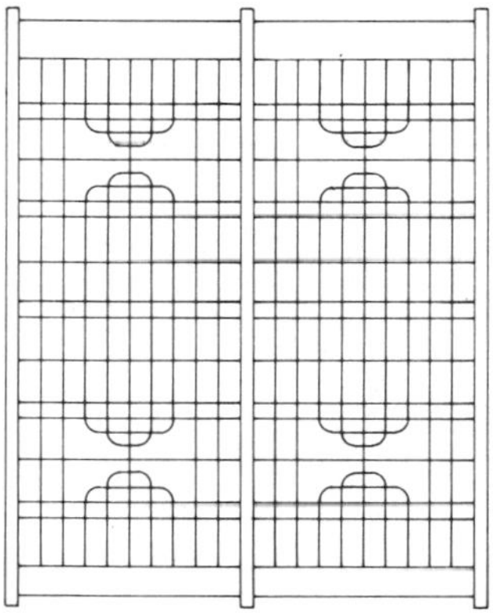
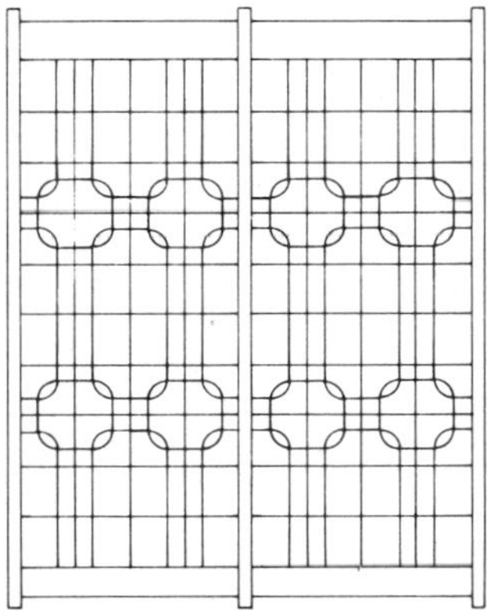
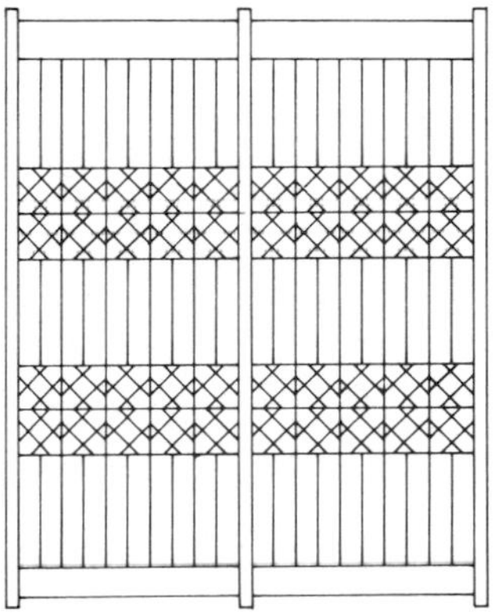
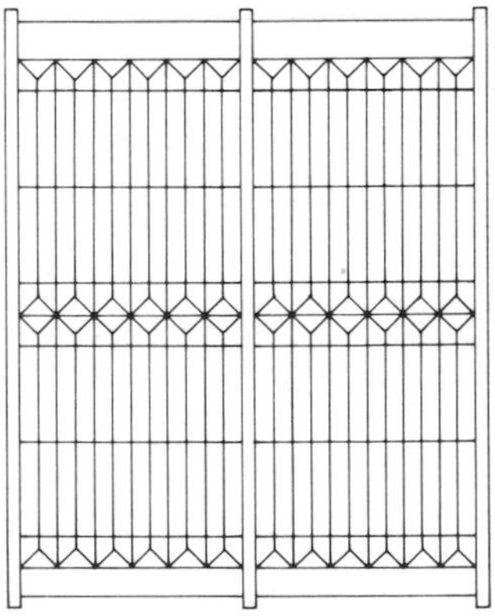
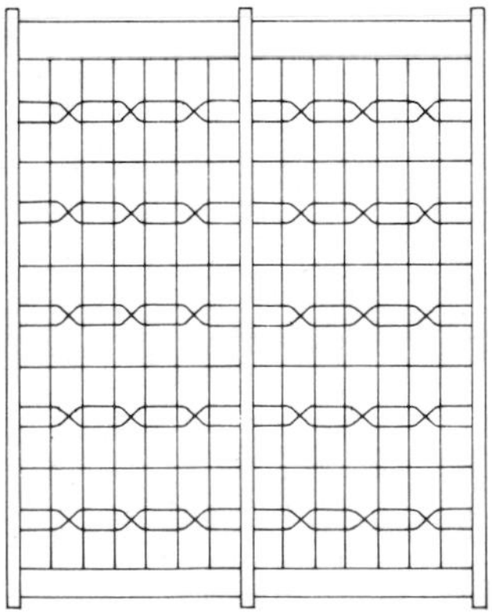
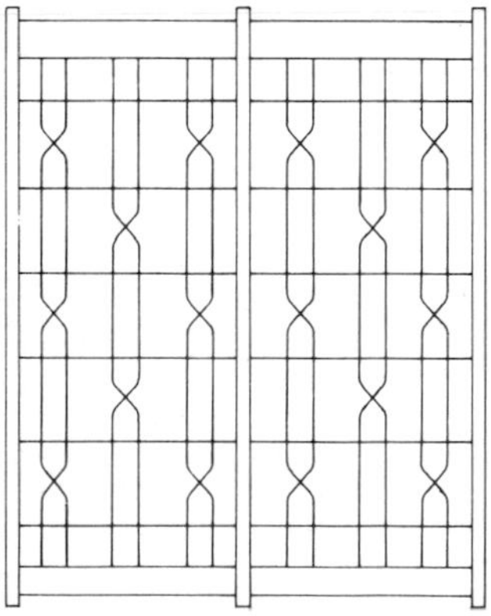

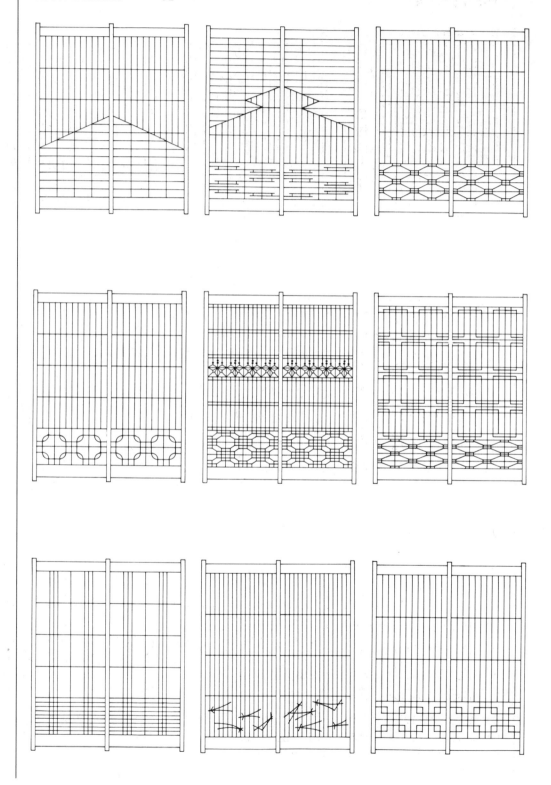

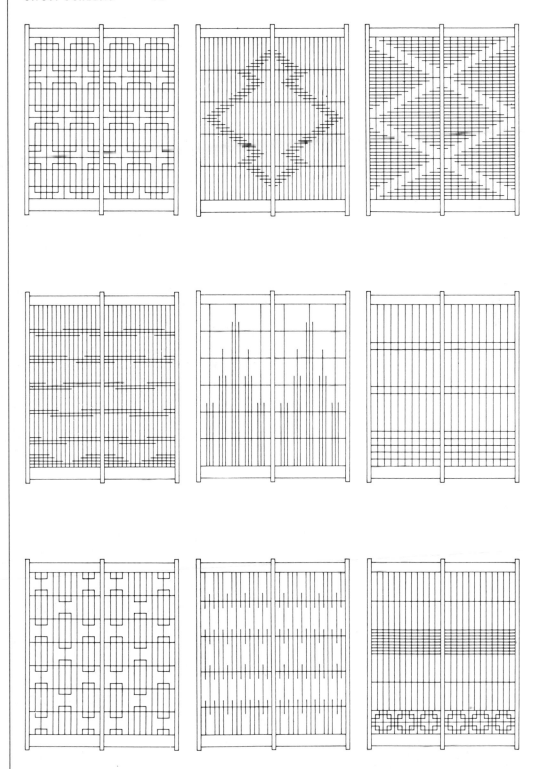

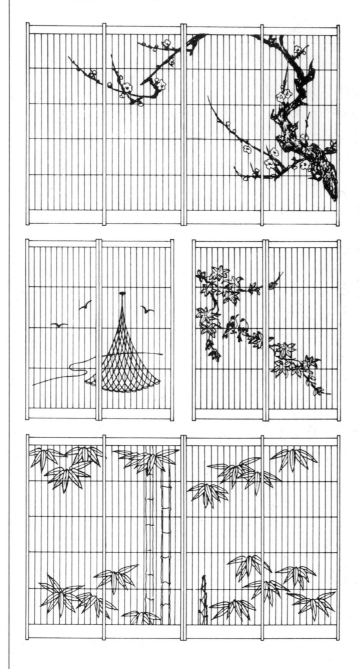

Full-length Shoji

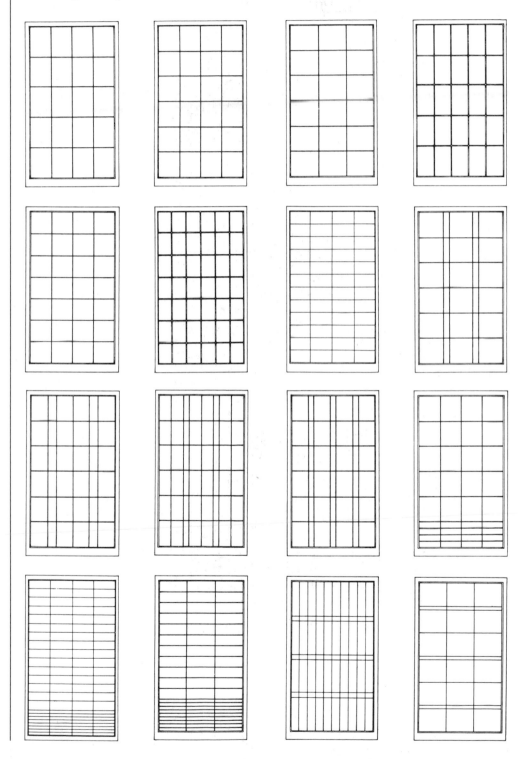

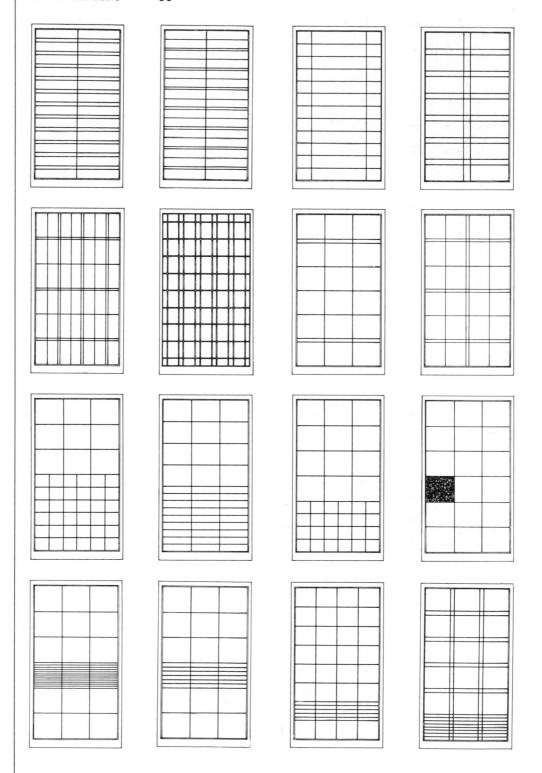

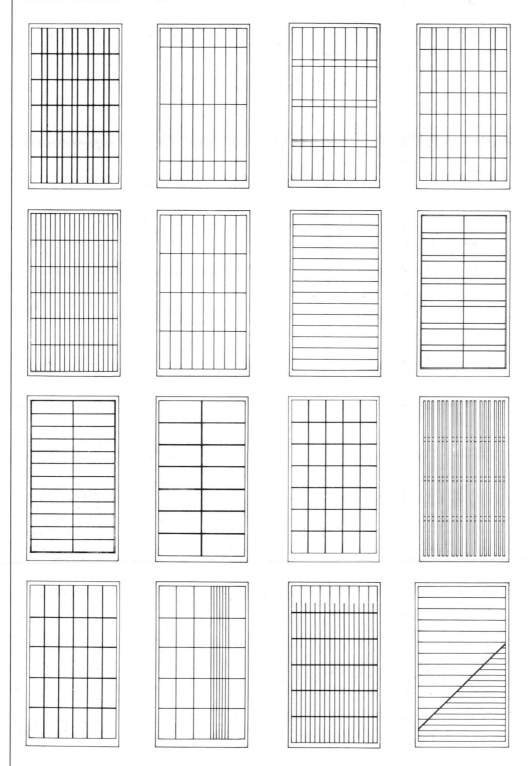

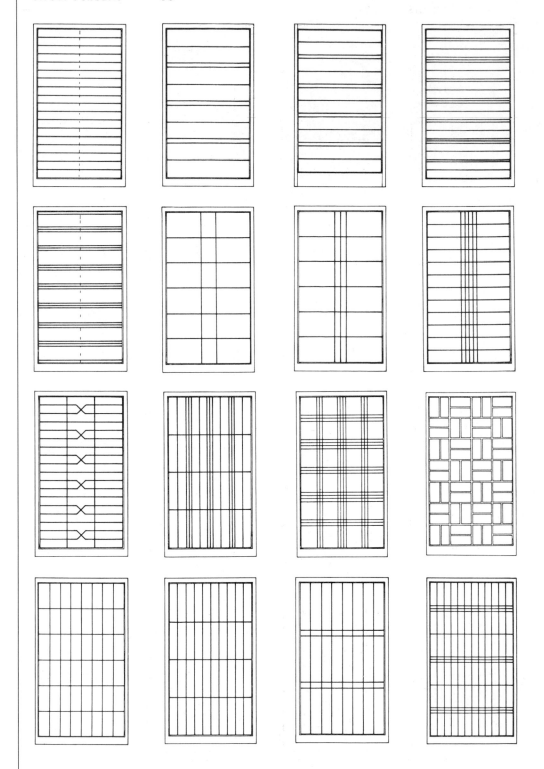

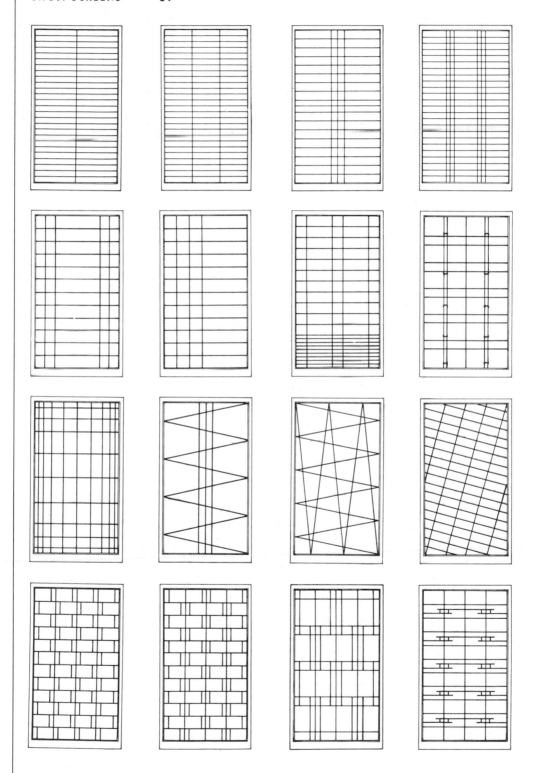

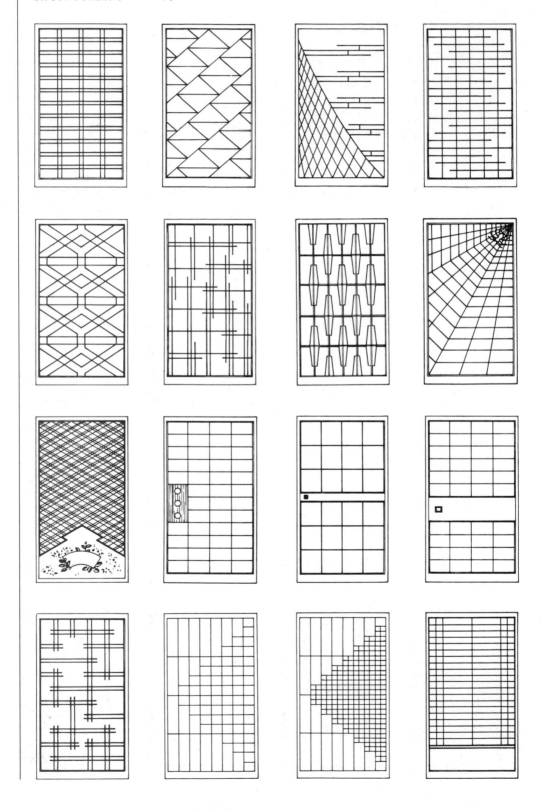

Shoji with Hipboards

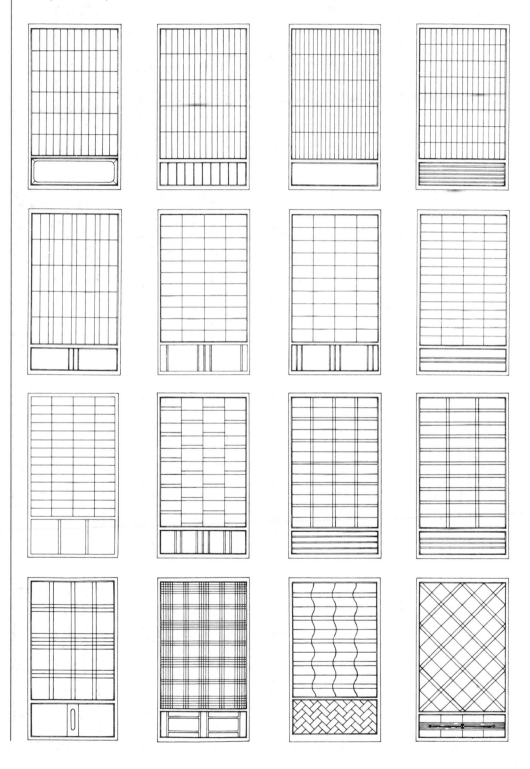

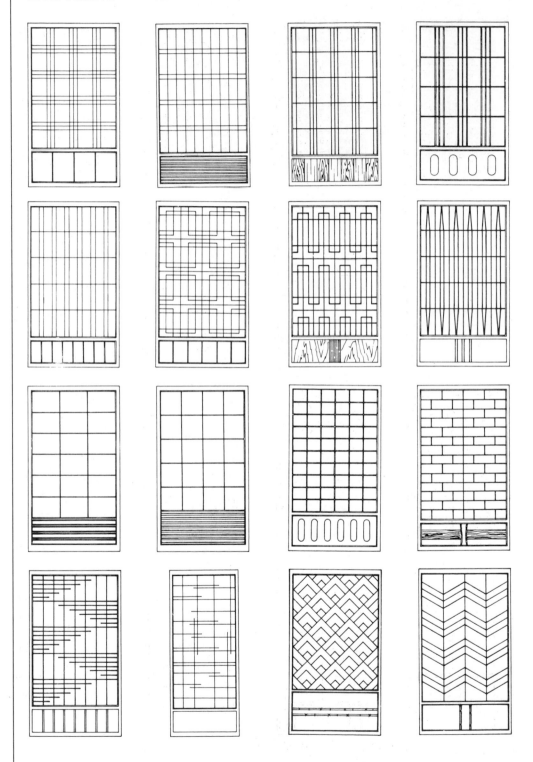

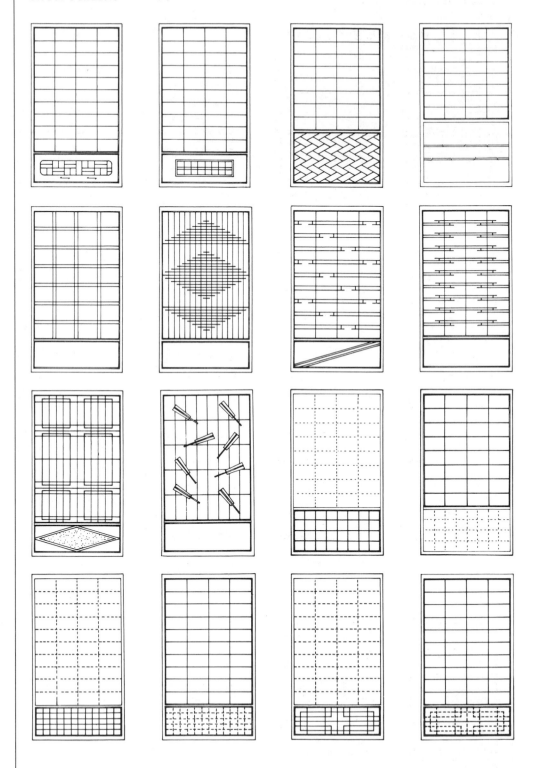

Shoji with Hipboards and Sliding Panels

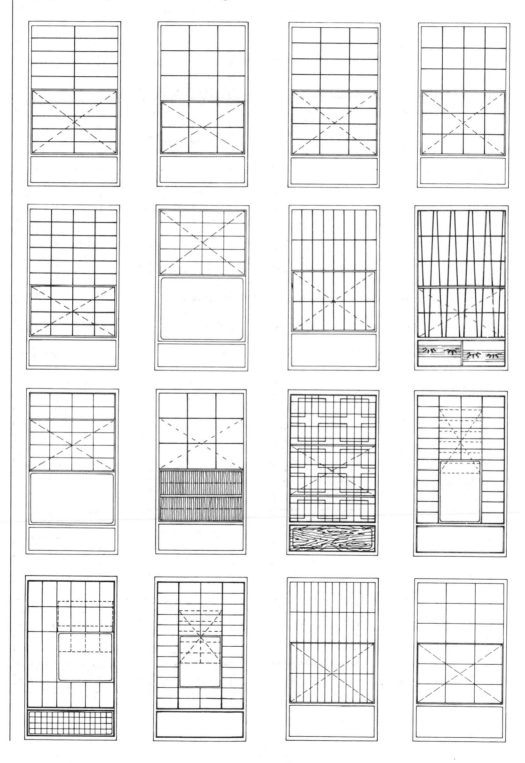

Shoji with Sliding Panels and No Hipboards

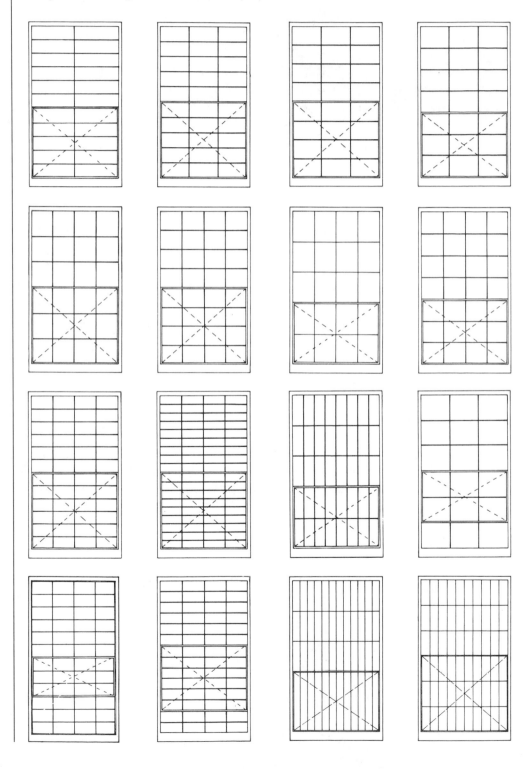

Shoji with Glass Panel Inserts

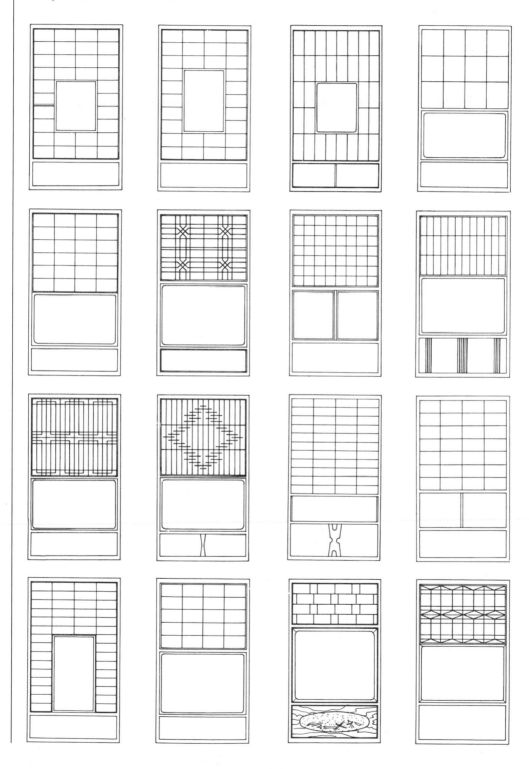

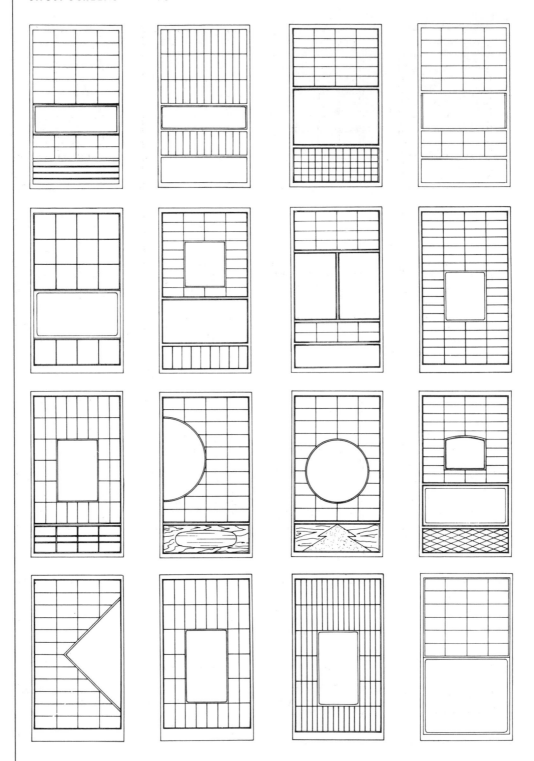

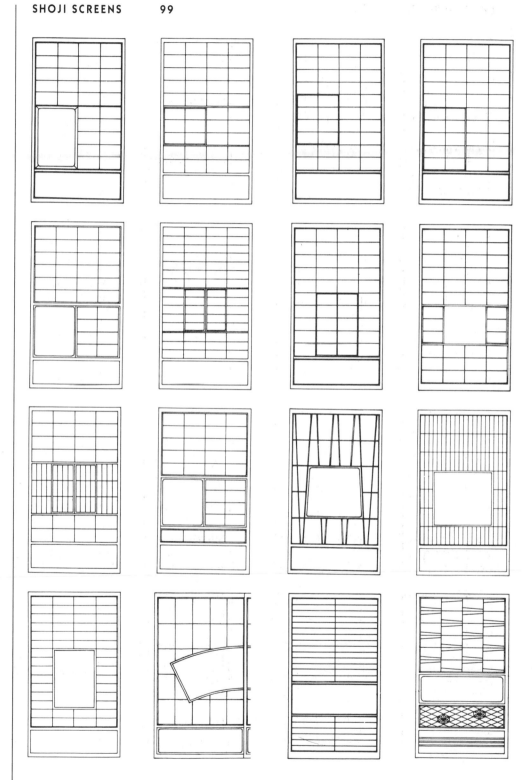

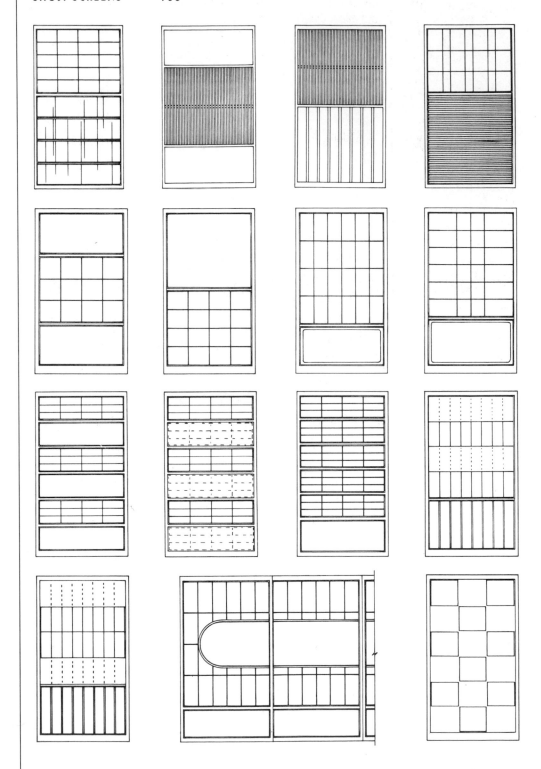

Functionally, Japanese windows are like shoji in that they use transmitted light to carry a strong graphic design element into the interior room of the room. The window "pane" is traditionally made of paper, but unlike shoji, most Japanese windows do not open (although a window may be fitted with sliding shoji on its opposite side). Many of the designs in this chapter are for windows above the benchlike writing desk near the tokonoma alcove. Some windows are installed low to the ground so that they are best admired from a seated position. Windows consisting of open pass-throughs and a simple reed lattice but no paper (or glass) epitomize the peasant aesthetic associated with the tea ceremony.

Window Shapes

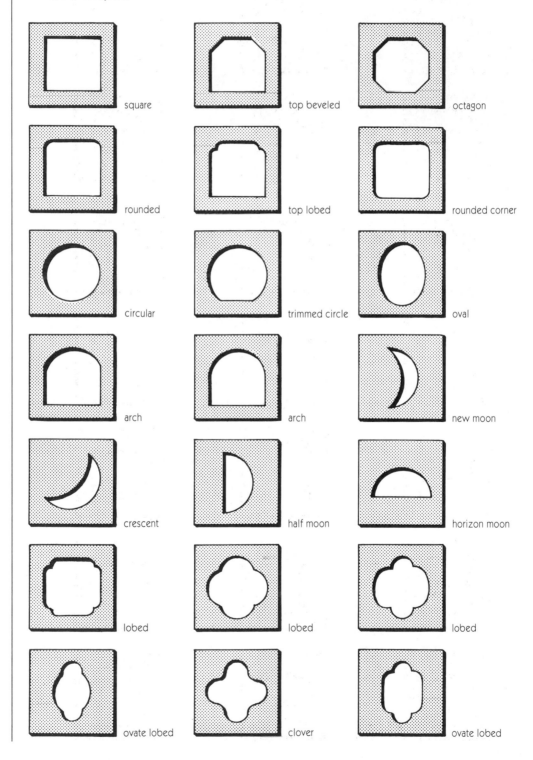

square

top beveled

octagon

rounded

top lobed

rounded corner

circular

trimmed circle

oval

arch

arch

new moon

crescent

half moon

horizon moon

lobed

lobed

lobed

ovate lobed

clover

ovate lobed

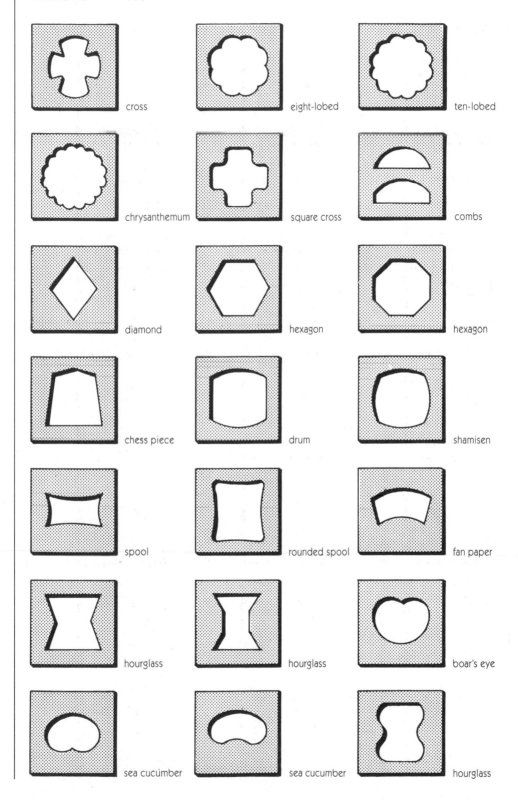

cross

eight-lobed

ten-lobed

chrysanthemum

square cross

combs

diamond

hexagon

hexagon

chess piece

drum

shamisen

spool

rounded spool

fan paper

hourglass

hourglass

boar's eye

sea cucumber

sea cucumber

hourglass

gourd

 stacked and trimmed circles

 bird's egg

 saddle flap

 scooped ellipse

 Mt. Fuji

 plum

 cherry blossom

 maple leaf

 origami crane

 mist

 vertical pine-bark rhombuses

 tiered diamond

 loophole

 flying birds

 zigzag star

 cut-bamboo cross

 pestles

 gourd

 butterfly

 flying butterfly

Weave Variations

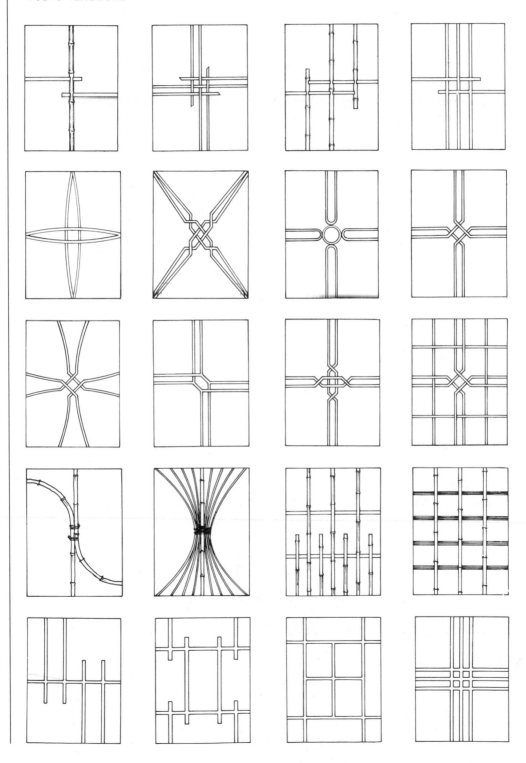

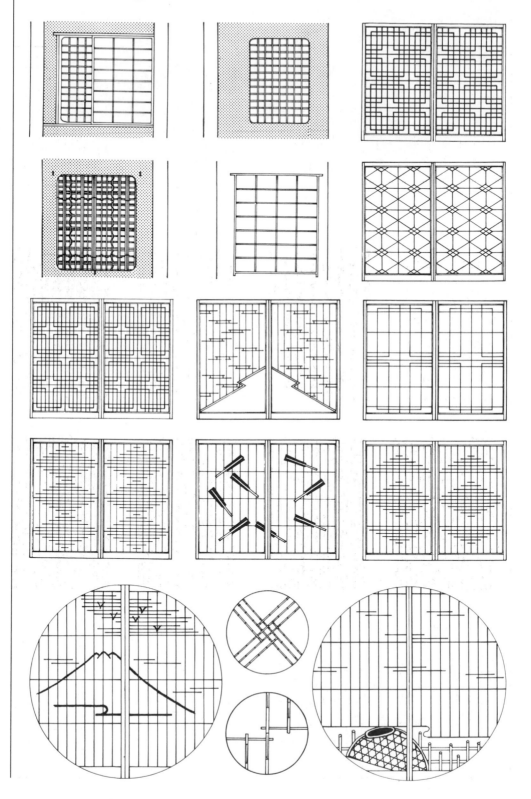

Lattice Patterns

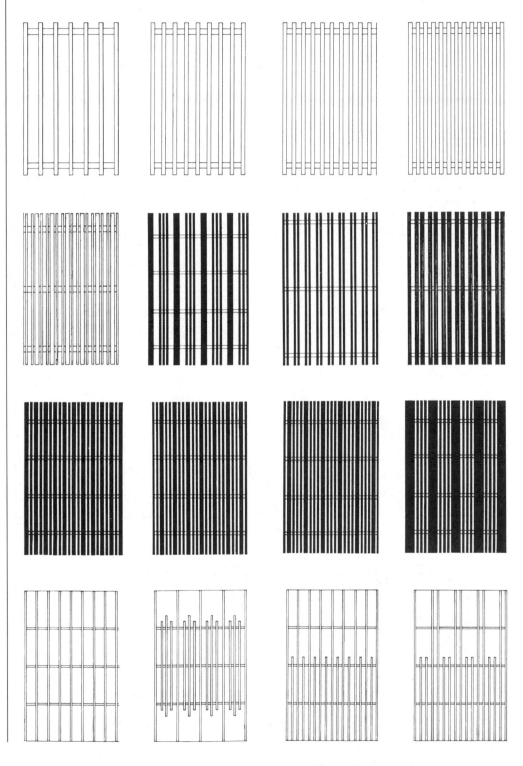

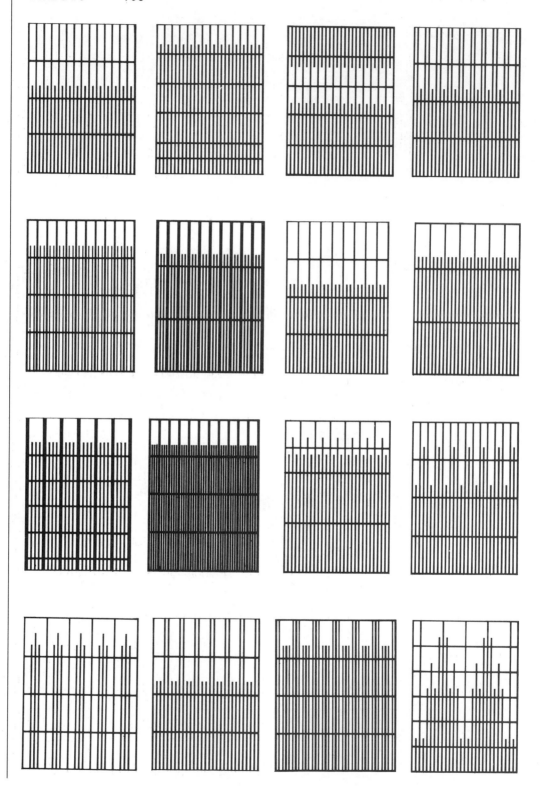

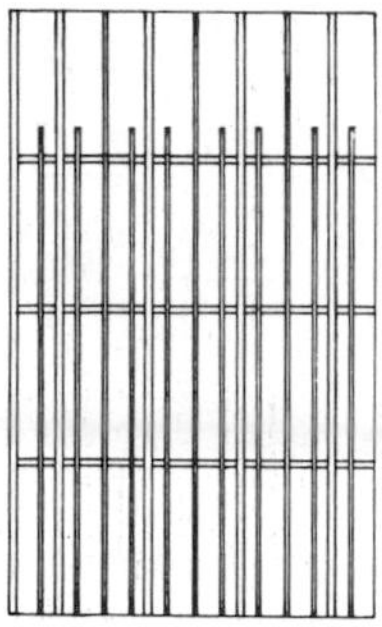
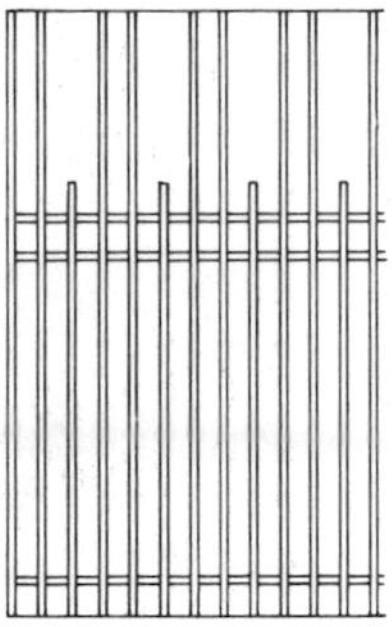
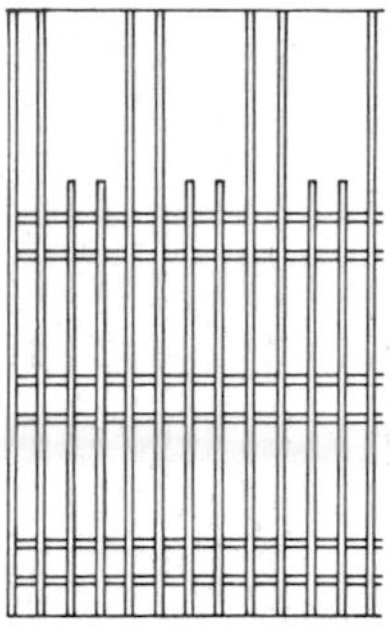
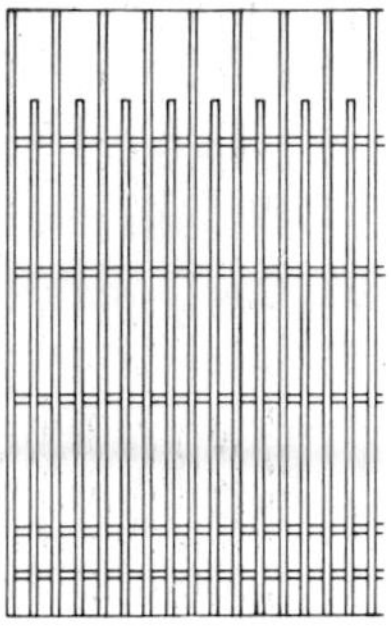
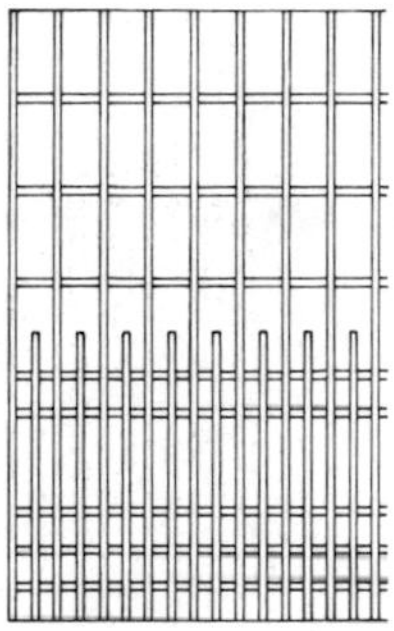
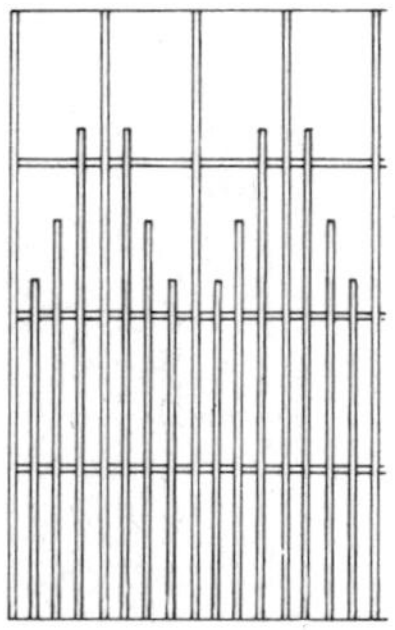
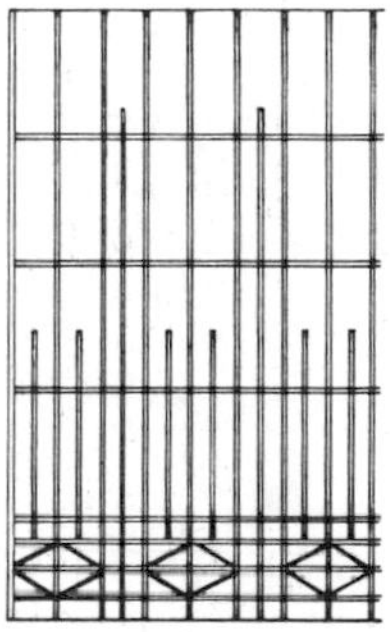
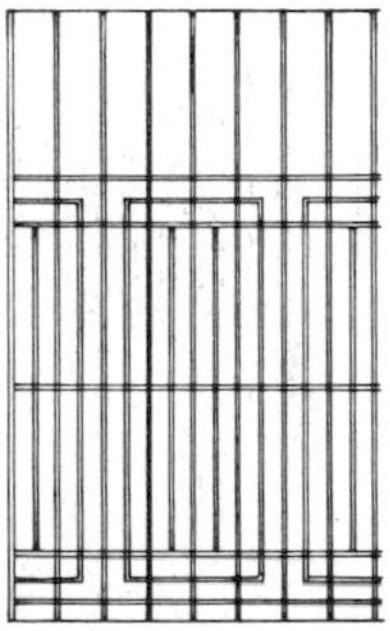
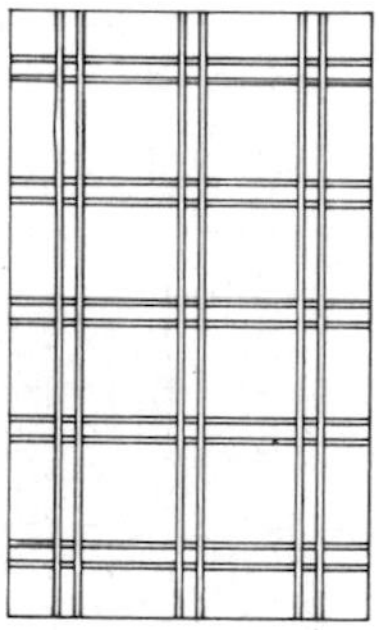
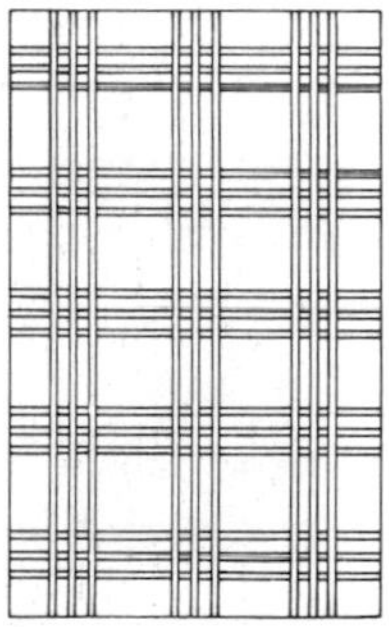
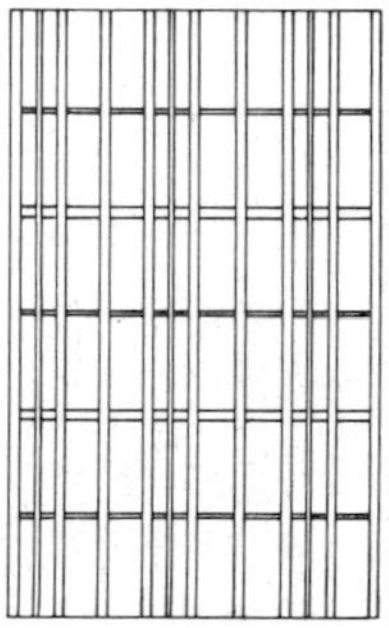
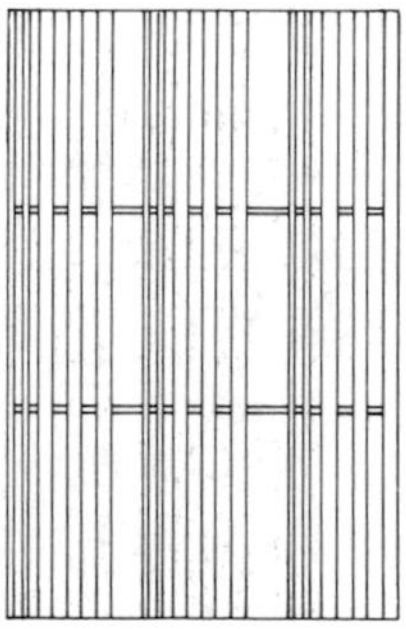
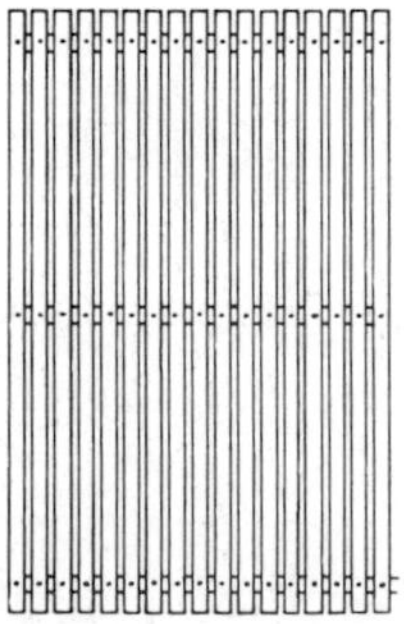
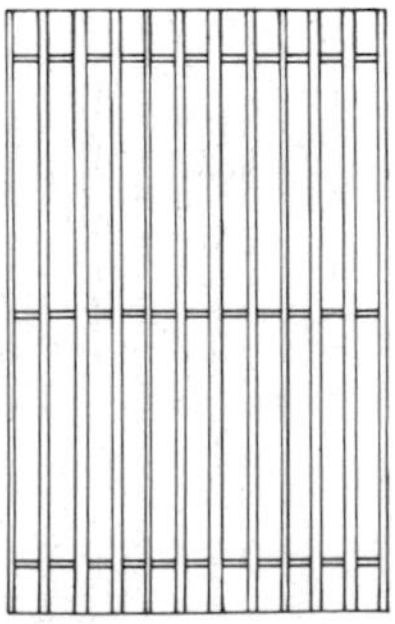
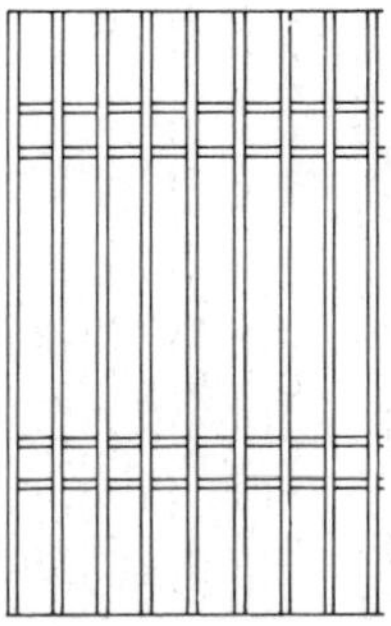
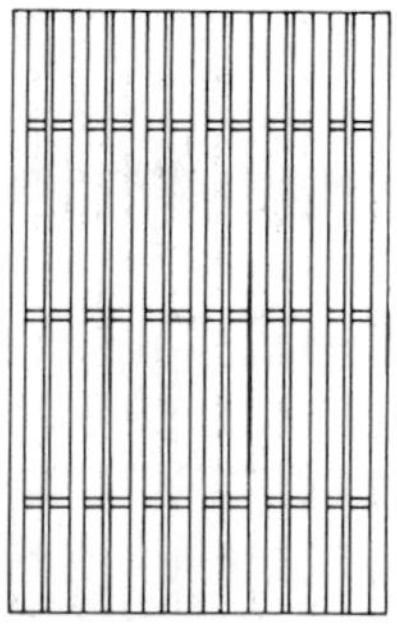

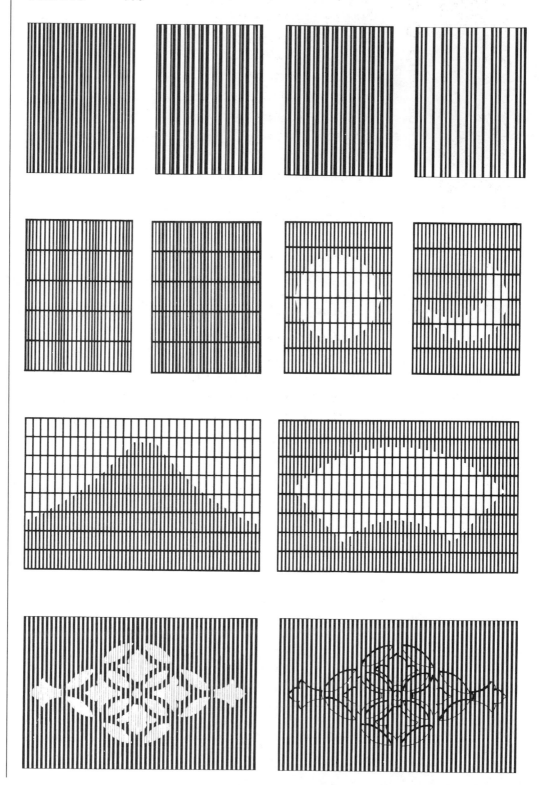

Japanese doors are not hinged but slide in tracks like shoji and fusuma screens. An entryway door is actually well inside the property—one must pass through a gate and then along a path before reaching it—so it provides less security than privacy and insulation. Doors are also used for bathrooms and washrooms. The quality of a door design depends first on the relative size and spacings of the horizontal and vertical elements, and next on the surface texture of the wood itself. Japanese planing brings out the wood's natural luster to fine decorative effect. Cedar is favored for its ability to resist insects and weathering. Doors can be fitted with glass or reeds. Some are solid boards with carved or chamfered crosspieces.

Doors with Decorative Crosspieces

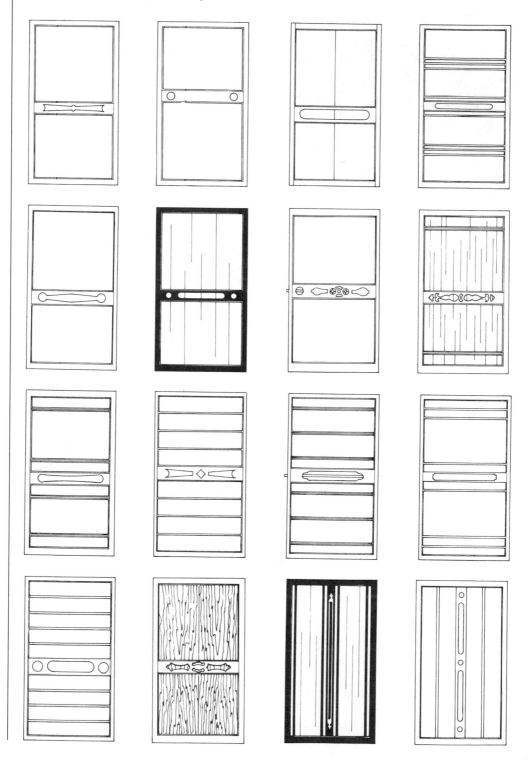

Doors with Slats

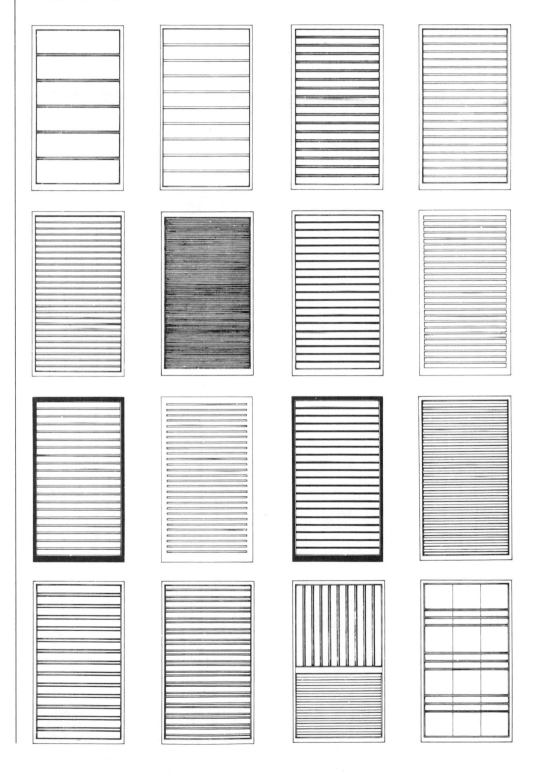

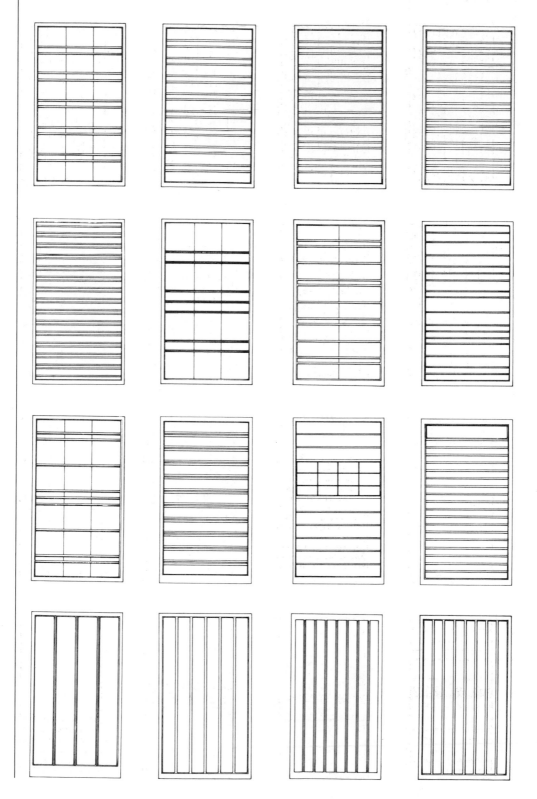

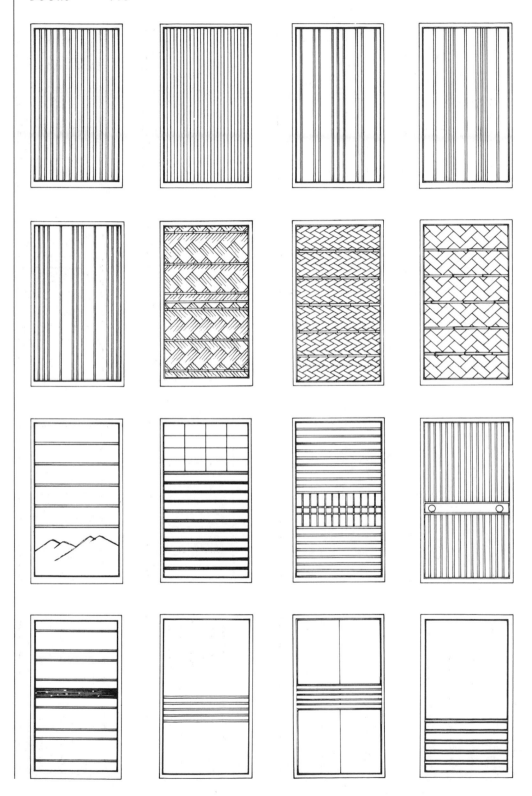

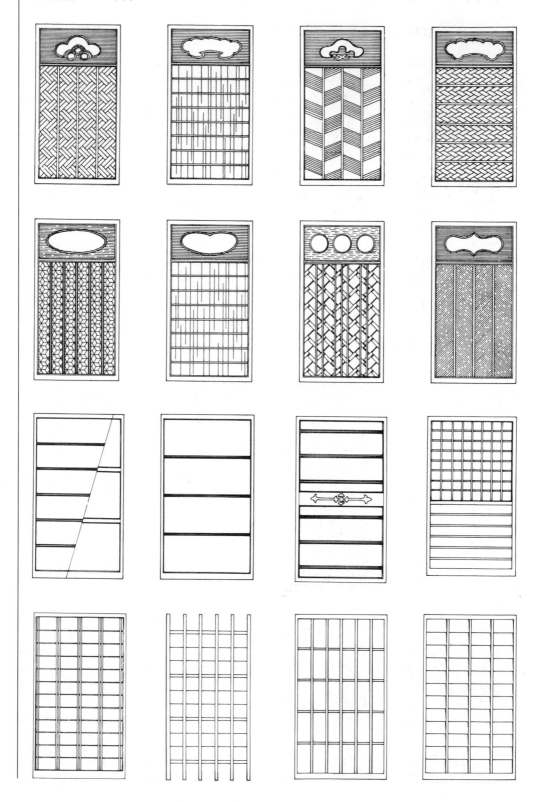

Bamboo and Reed Doors

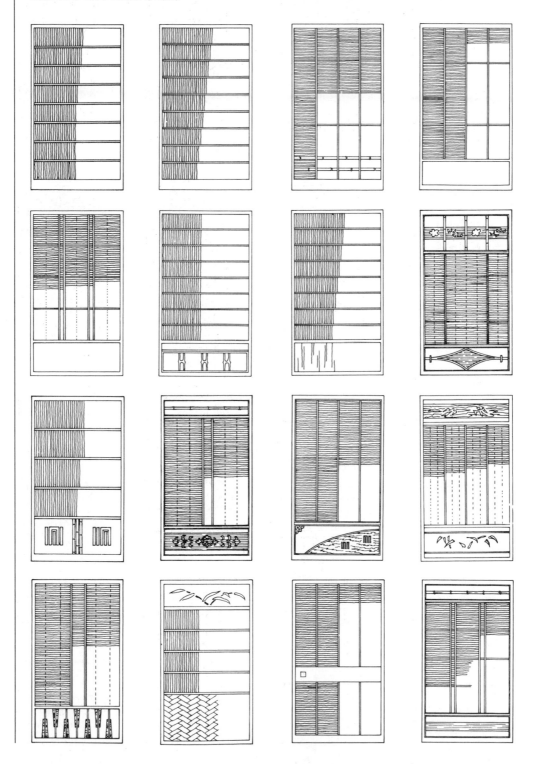

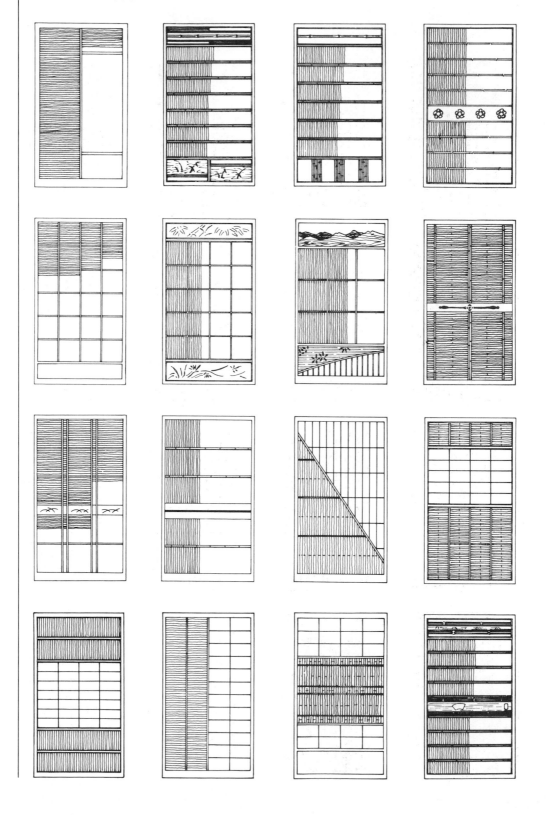

Lattice Doors

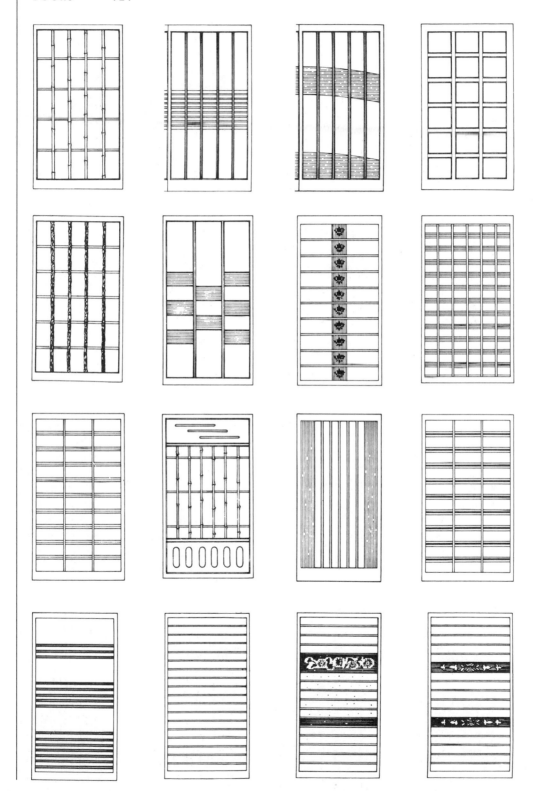

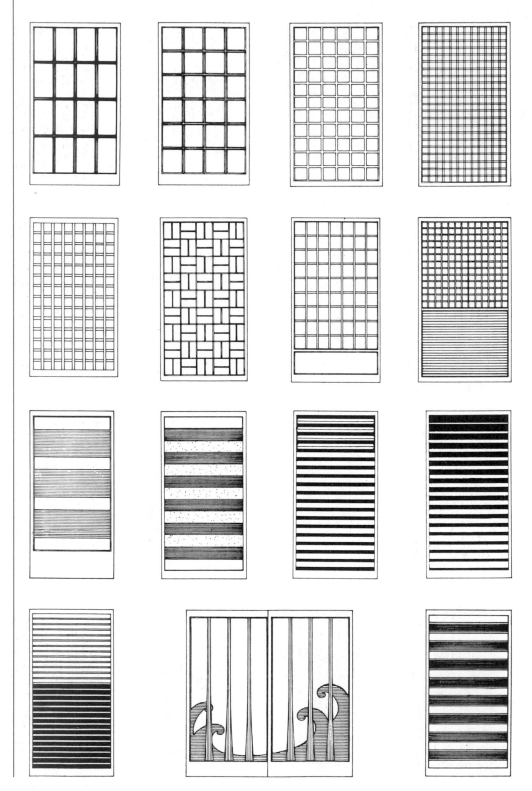

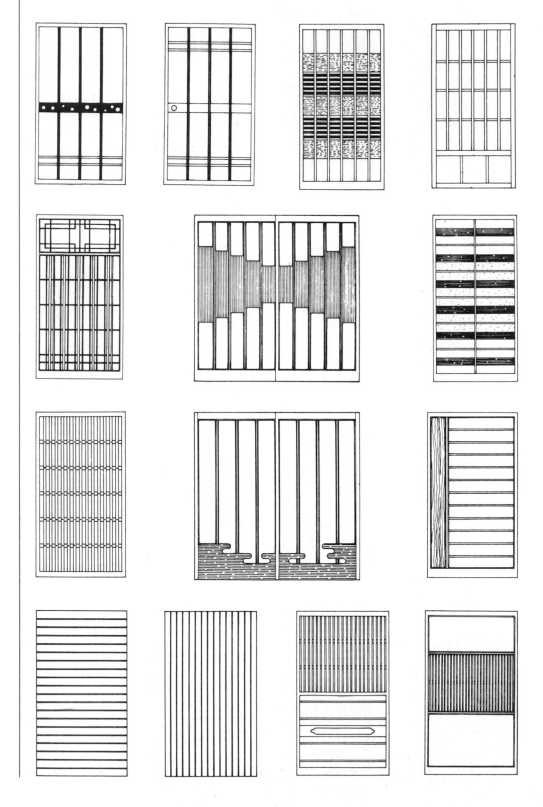

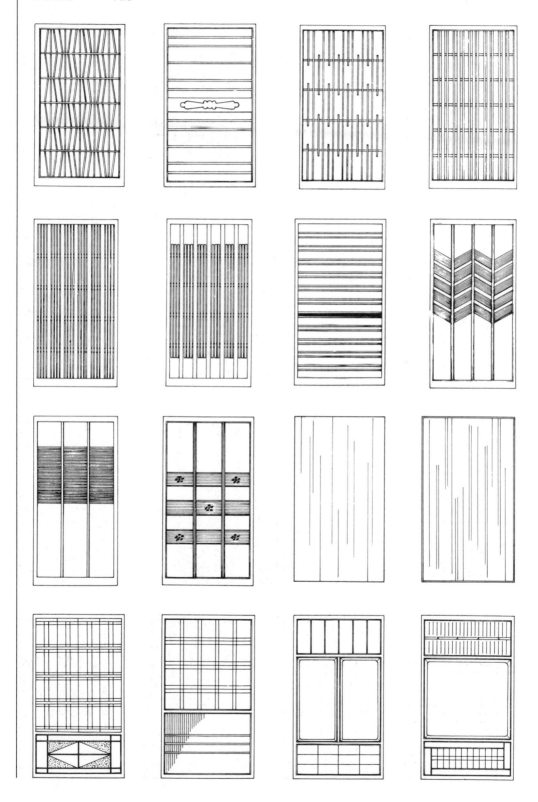

"Osaka-style" Doors (may have shoji backings)

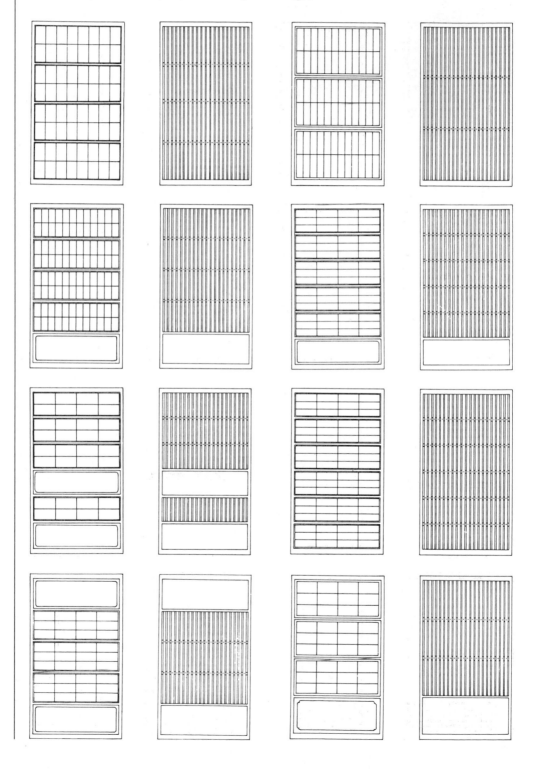

Doors with Glass Panels

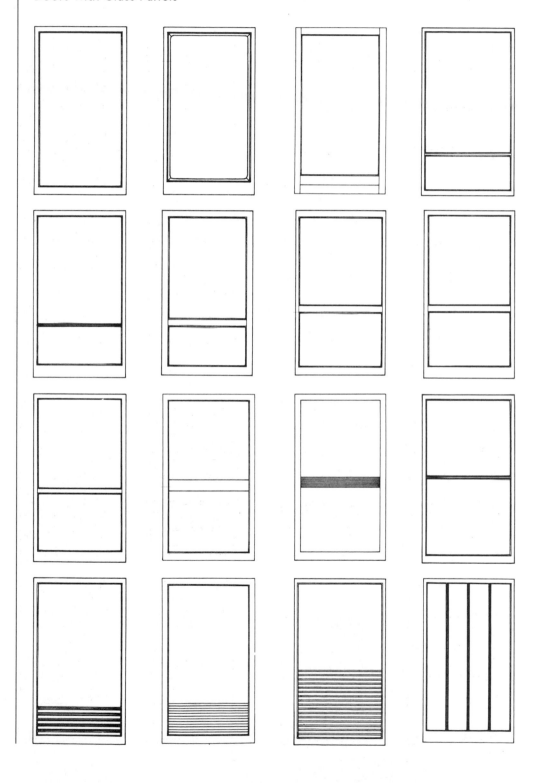

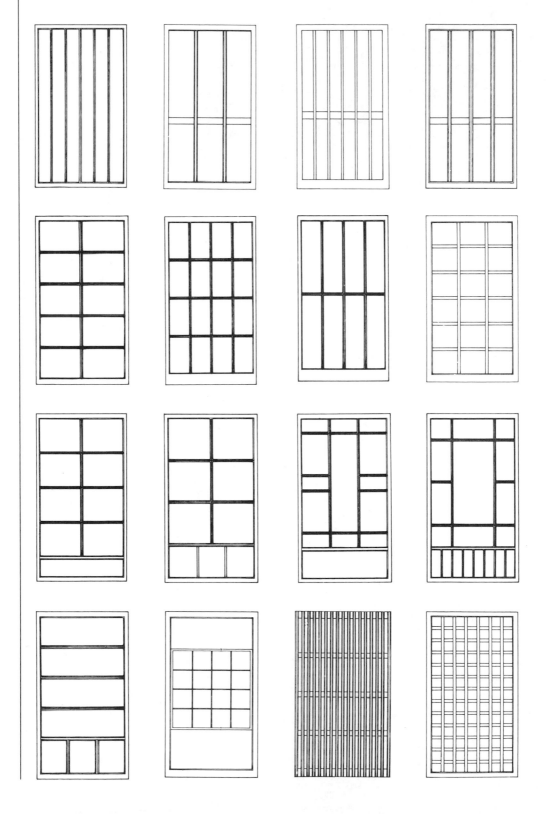

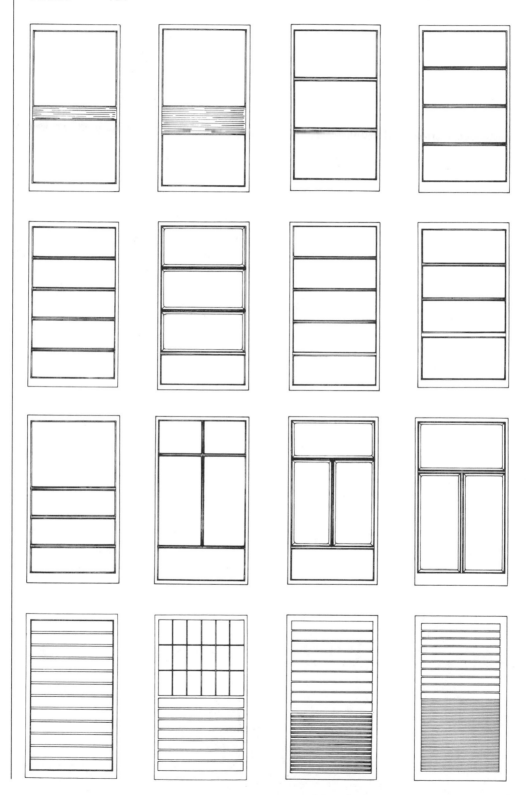

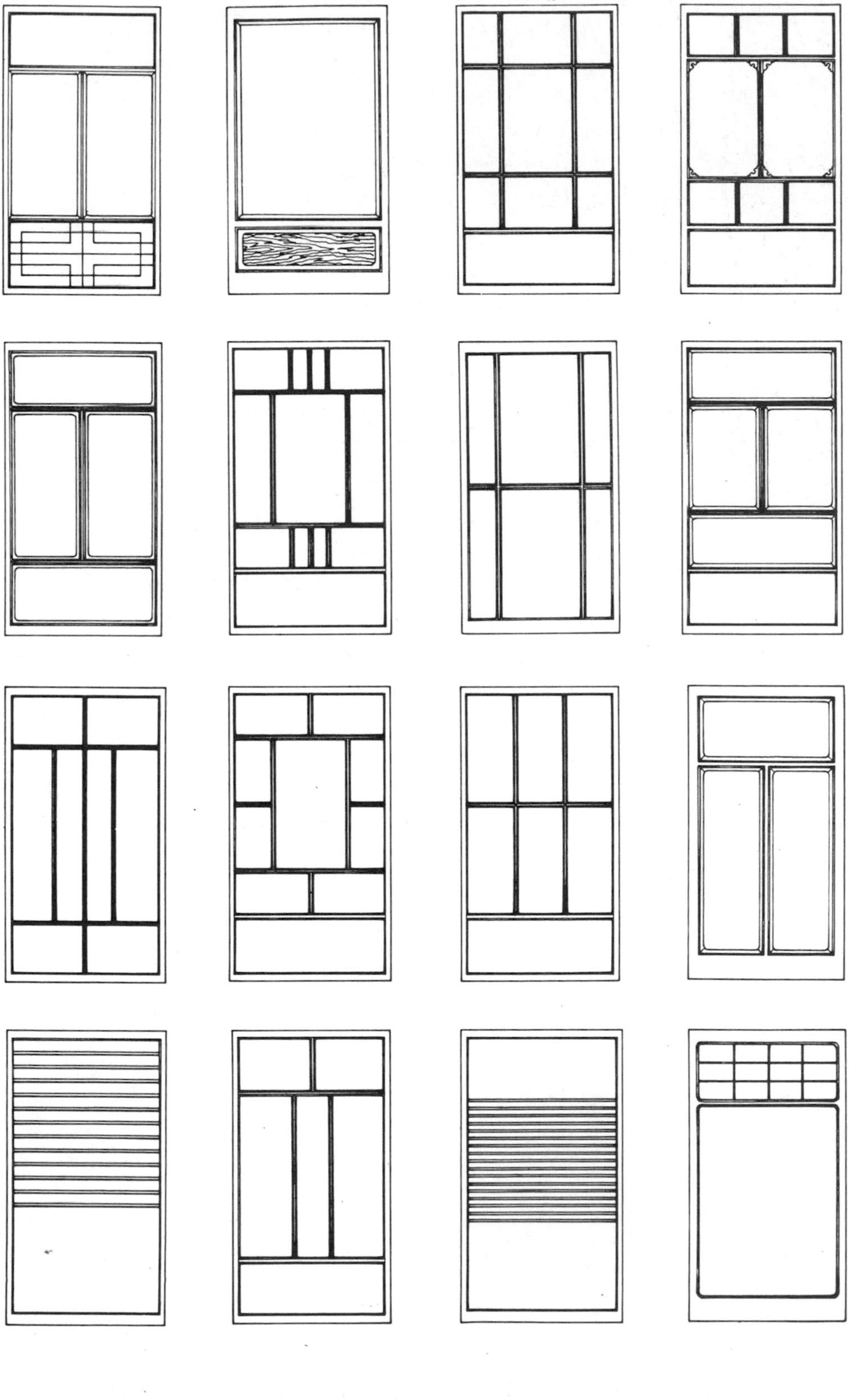

RAILINGS AND VERANDAS

Traditional Japanese homes may be surrounded by a veranda (*engawa*), about 3 to 5 feet wide and 18 inches off the ground. This area is spatially a transitional zone. Connected directly to the room when the shoji are open, and tucked under the long eaves of the roof, it is interior and in fact functions as a corridor linking rooms along the entire length of the residence. Open to the elements, however, it is exterior. The breadth of the veranda protects the room shoji from direct exposure to rain and wind, but if necessary solid shutters can be installed in tracks along the veranda's outside edge. Railings are used for safety where necessary, and like transoms give the Japanese wood craftsman a chance to display his virtuosity. Decorative pavements can also serve as verandas at ground level.

Railing Designs

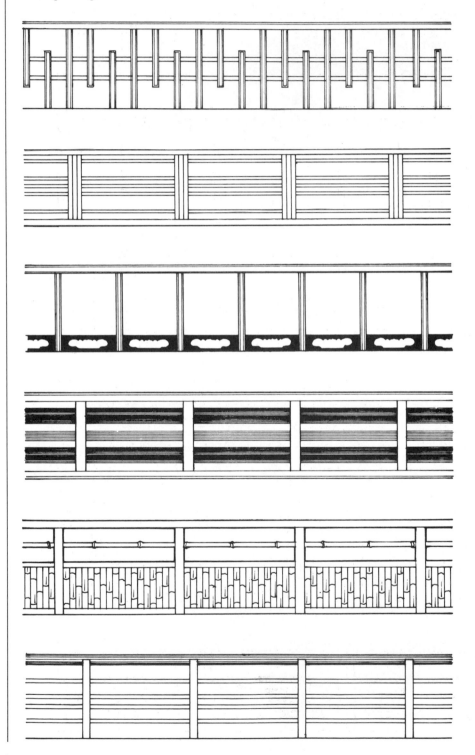

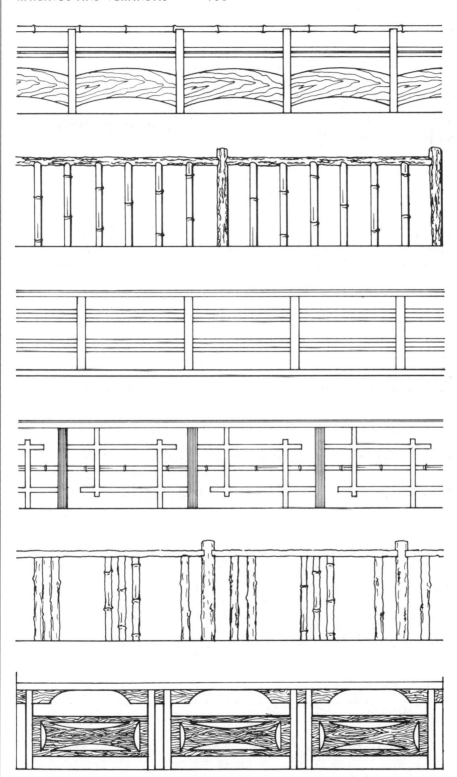

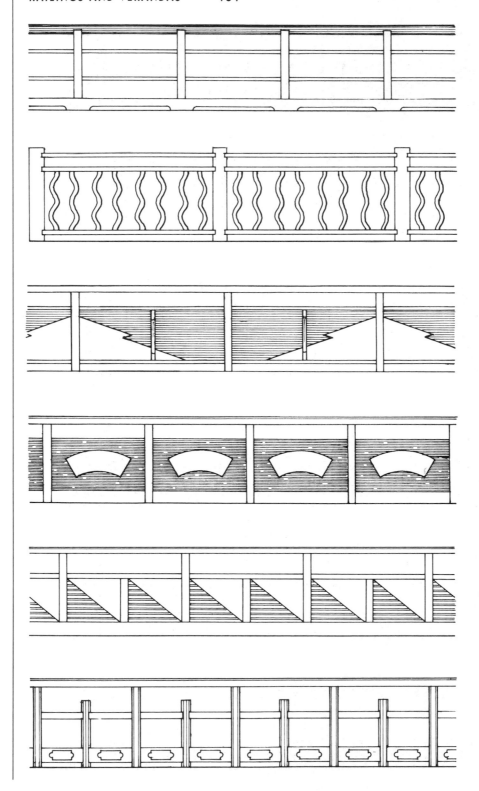

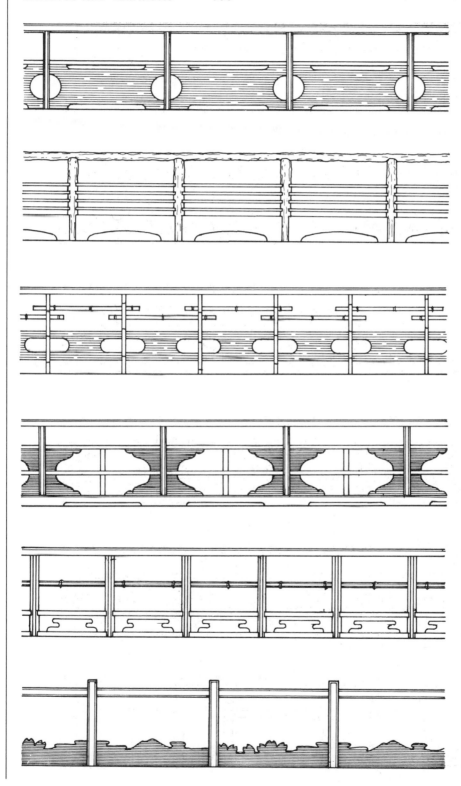

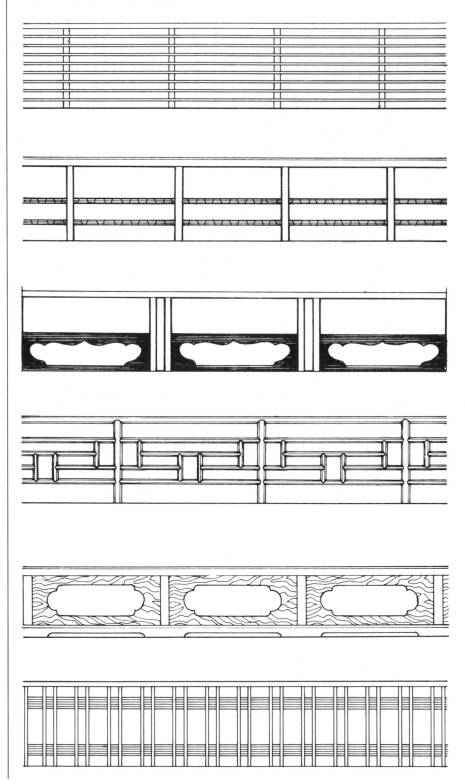

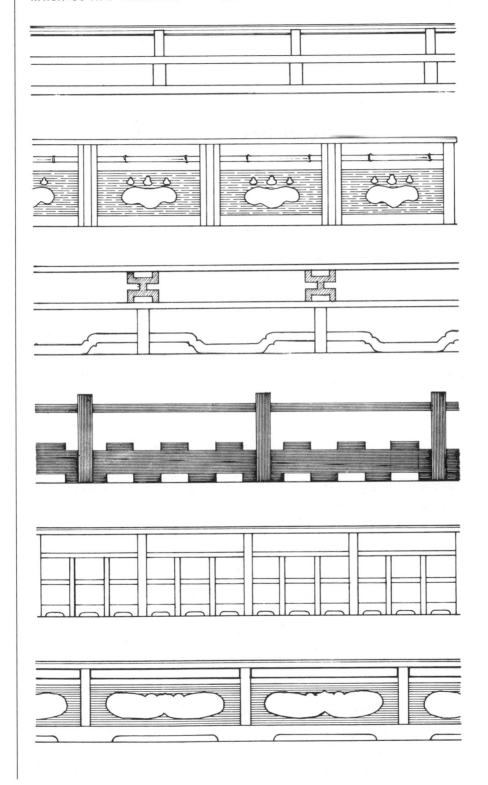

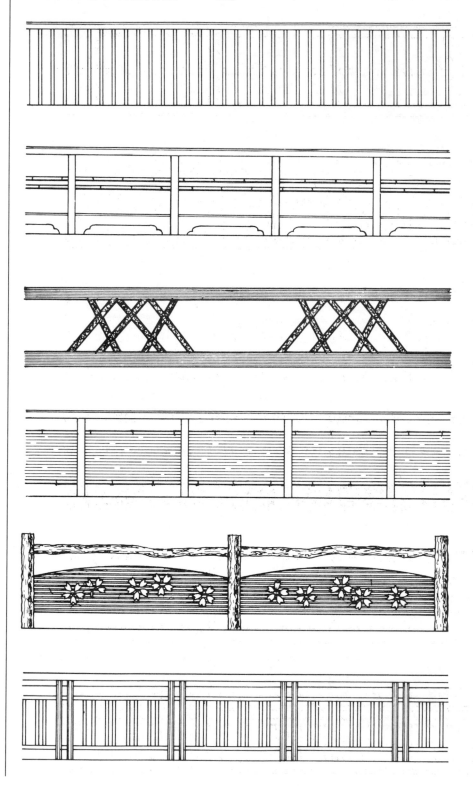

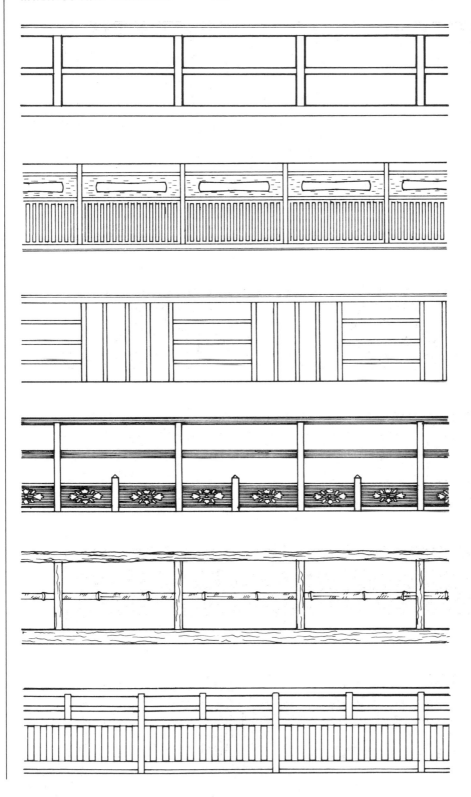

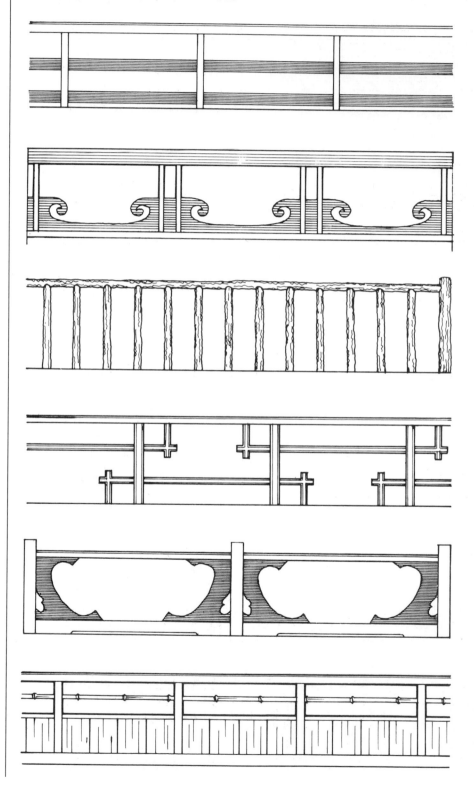

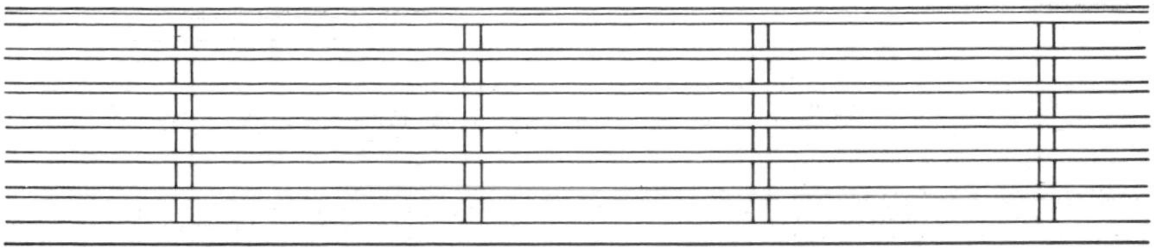

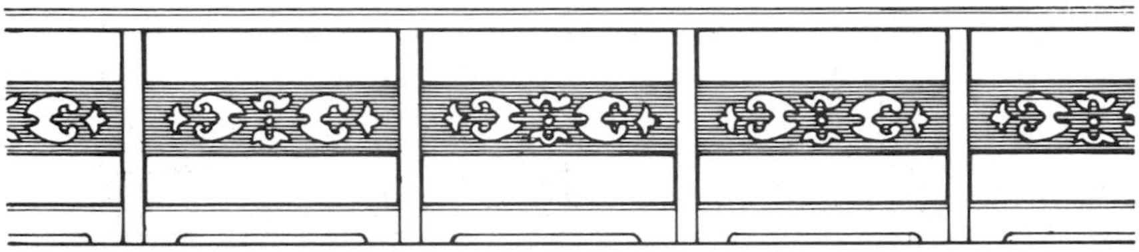

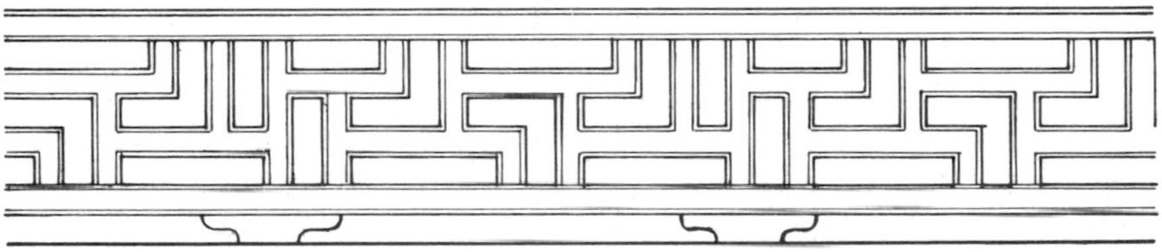

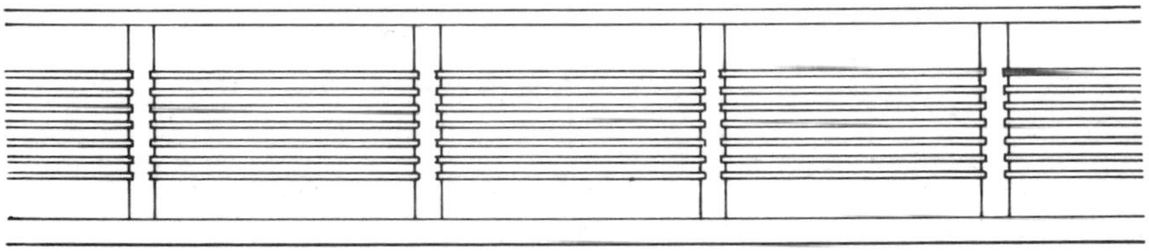

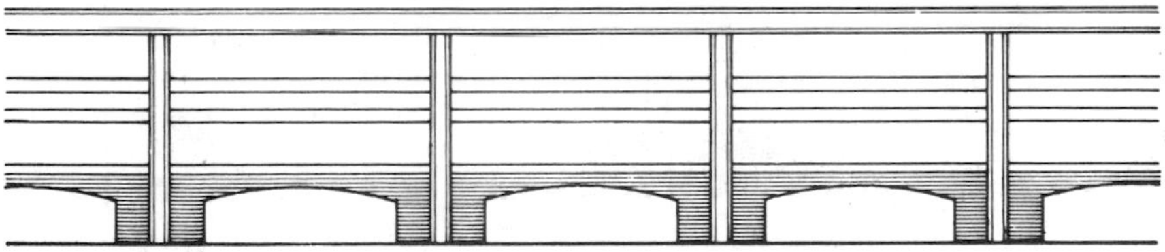

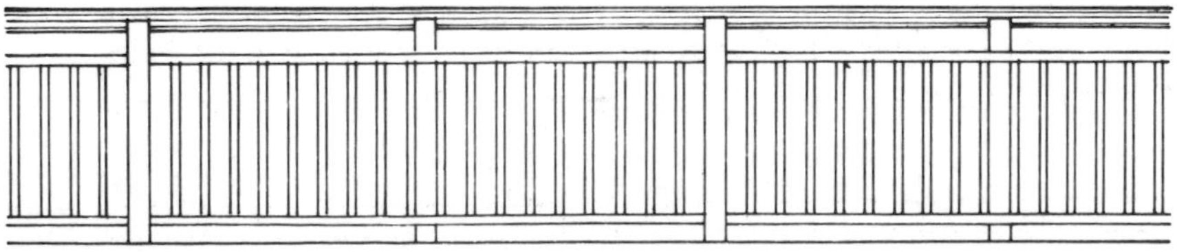

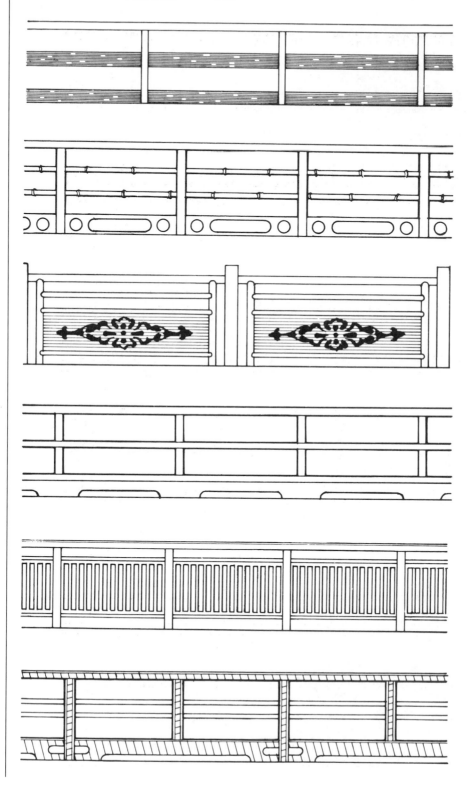

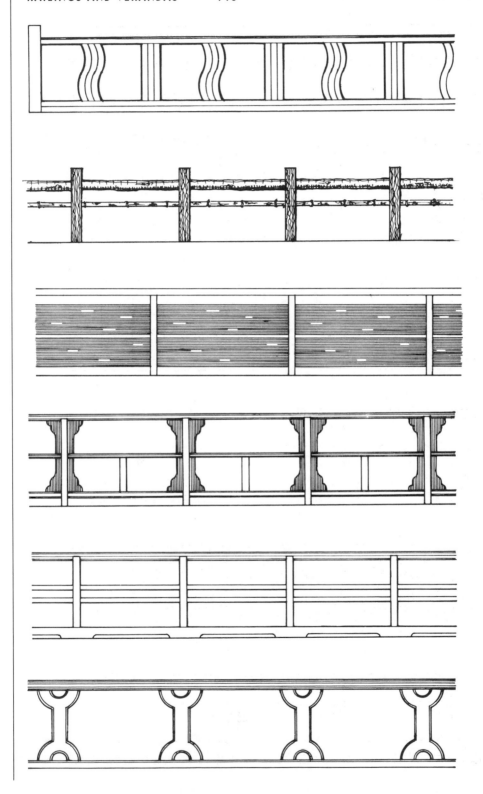

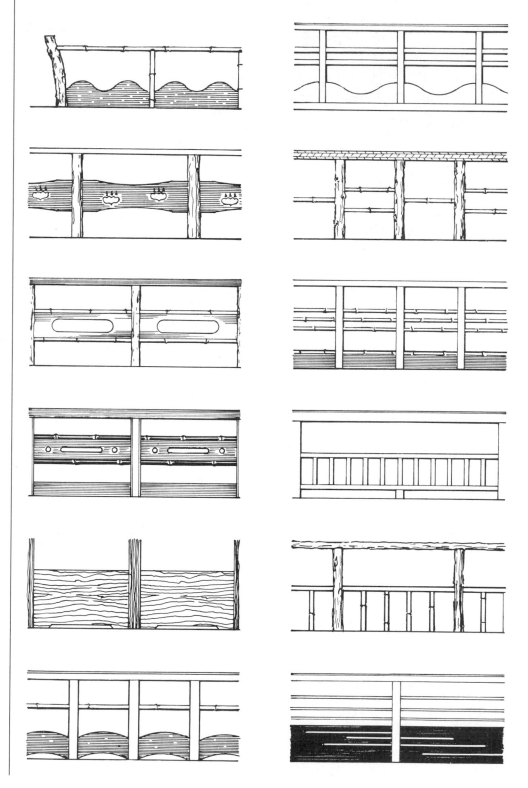

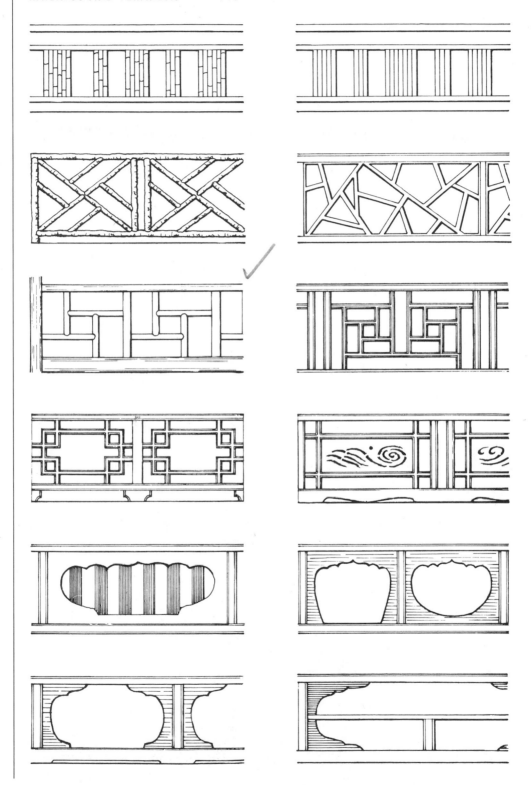

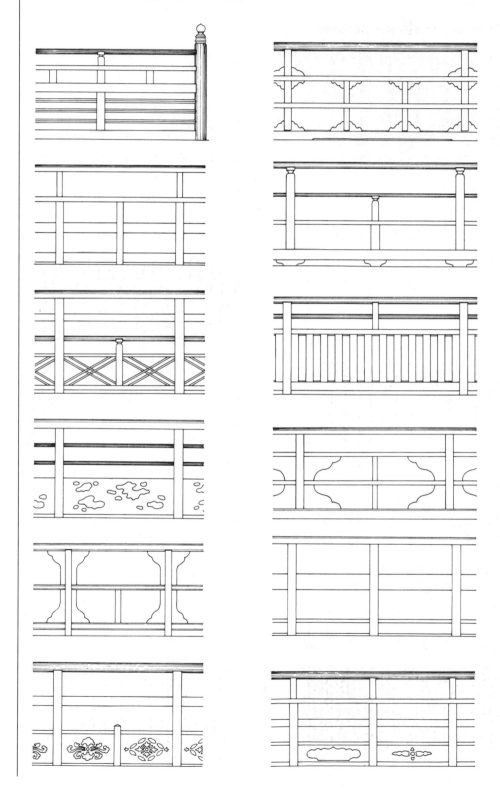

Veranda Textures and Designs

grooved

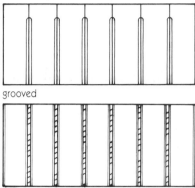

grooved

boards with open joins

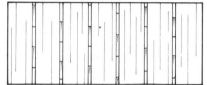

bamboo joins

beveled joins

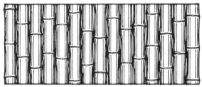

large split bamboo

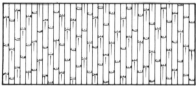

log and bamboo

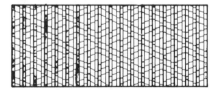

hexagonal adze-hewn pattern

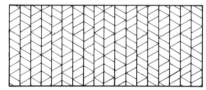

round bamboo

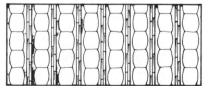

adze-hewn pattern

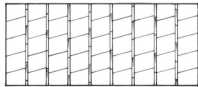

adze-hewn pattern

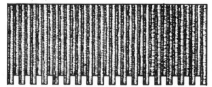

logs with shallow joins

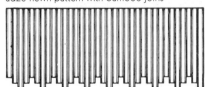

adze-hewn pattern with bamboo joins

square chamfer

planed logs

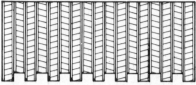

chamfered boards with adze-hewn pattern

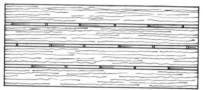

transverse bamboo joins

transverse groove

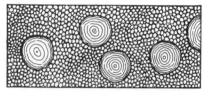

wood rounds and black stones

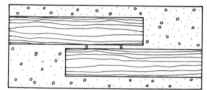

plank and gravel

wood rounds and pebbles

millstone, rock, and slab

adze-hewn pattern

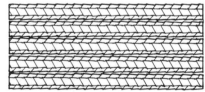

openwork adze-hewn pattern

millstone and rock

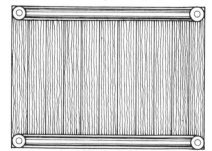

bridge planking

GARDEN FENCES AND PATHS

The Japanese consider that the "home" actually begins at the exterior wall of the property. Thus the garden is a part of one's everyday living space. Open shoji screens and the broad veranda visually bring the garden space into the house interior, through framing techniques and by extending the horizontal line of sight. Like gardens, fences are meant to be viewed, and many are built with rough, natural materials in accordance with the aesthetic of tea. The stone pathway or pavement leads the viewer through the garden: a smooth pavement allows you to walk comfortably while aware of the surrounding beauty, whereas an arrangement of spaced stones is used to fully occupy your attention until you are best positioned to admire a view or object. The mixing of formal and informal, scattered stone groupings in a single path is quite deliberate.

Fences of Bamboo, Split Bamboo, and Brushwood

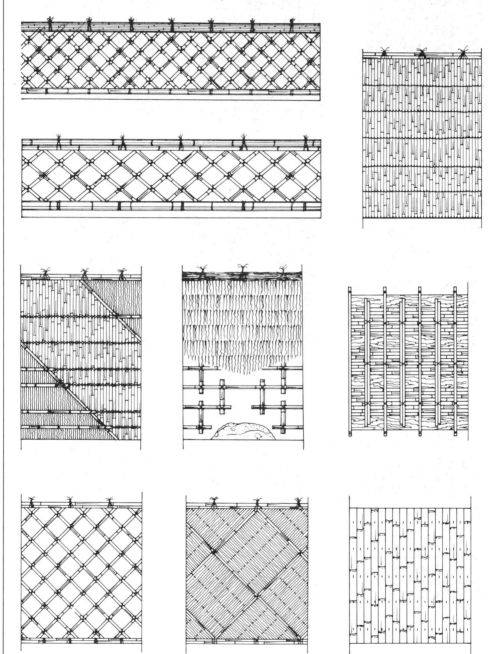

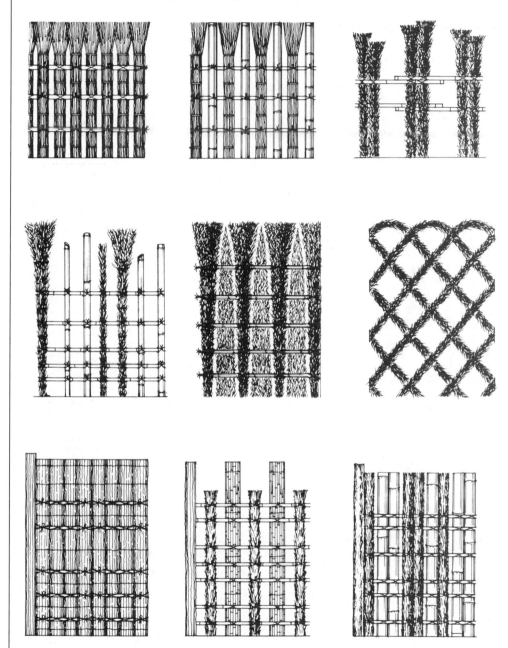

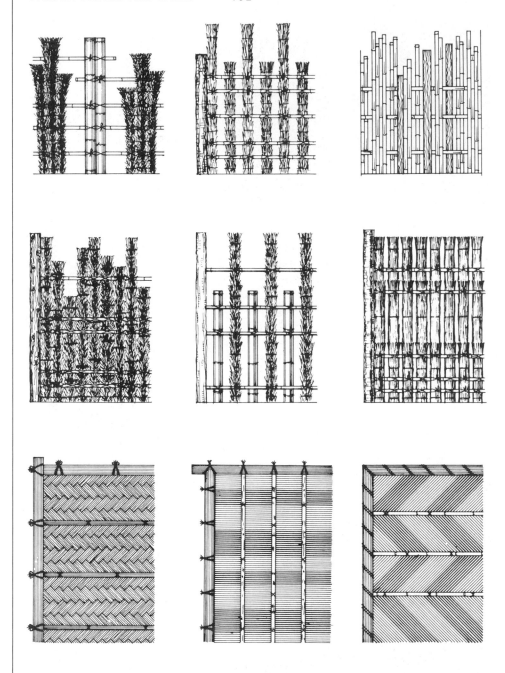

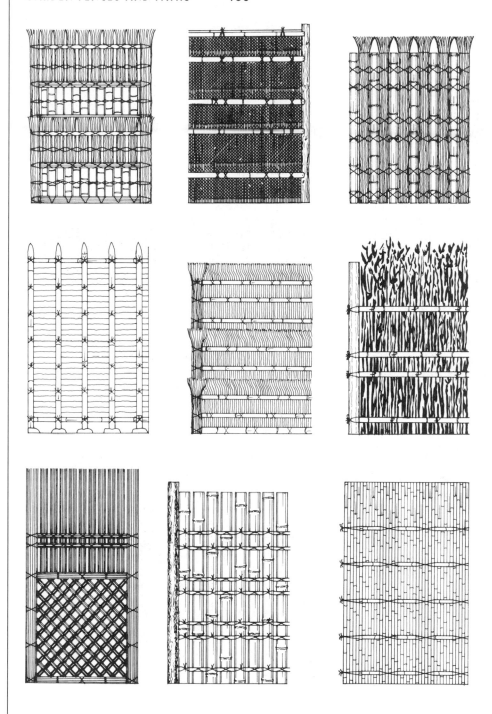

"Sleeve" (Screening) Fences of Bamboo, Brushwood, and Bush Clover

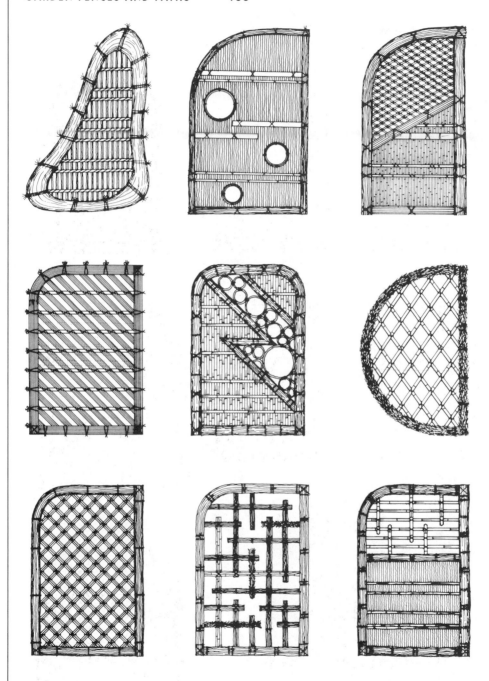

Pavement and Stepping Stone Designs

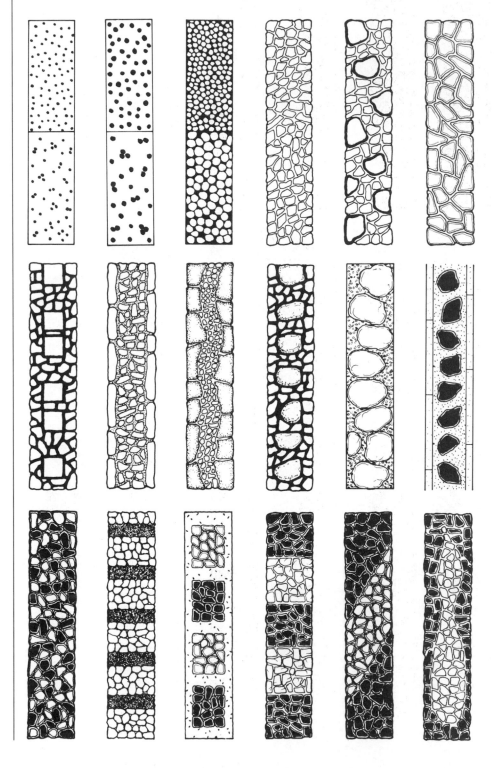

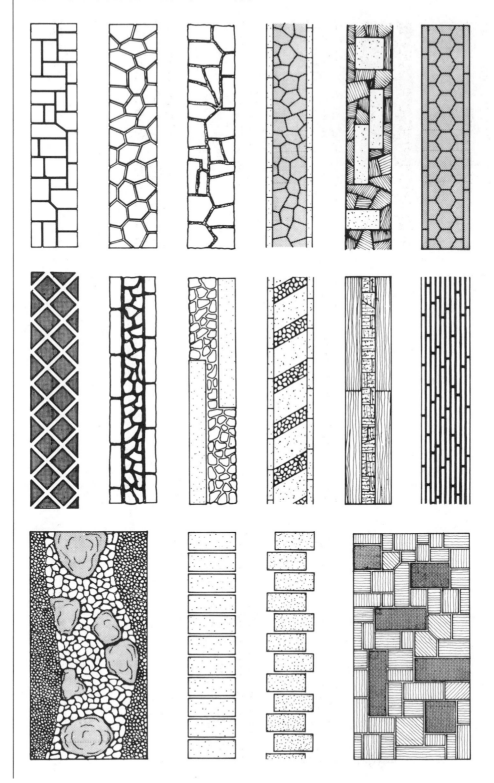

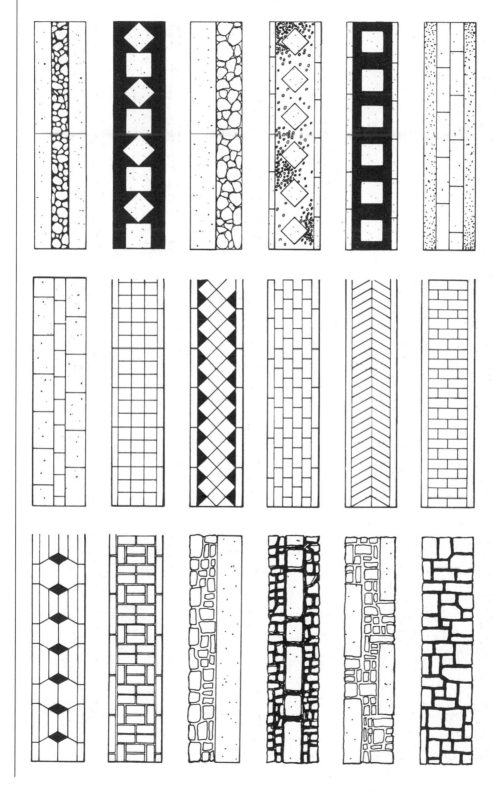

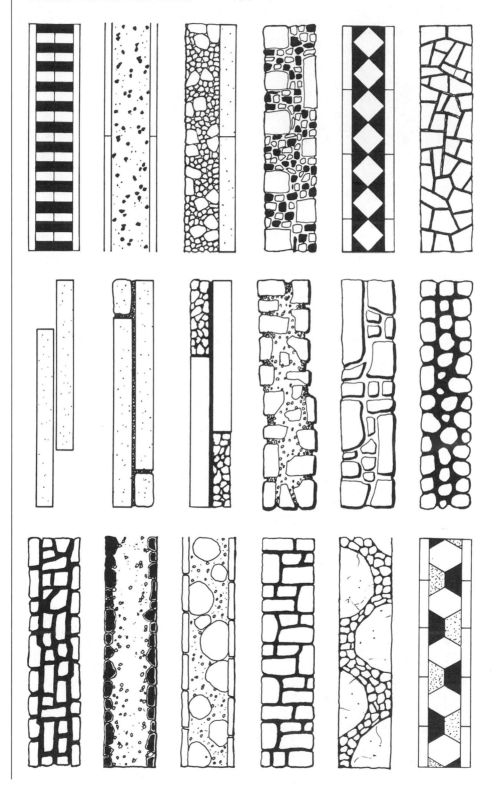

Collected on the following pages are some Japanese elements that can be used purely for their graphic value. The woven and lattice patterns used in Japanese architecture represent one type of "ironic" interlacing, where materials—reeds, rushes, wood, bamboo—are used in an unfinished natural state but combined in a way that is mathematical or logical. This may explain why Japanese homes are so aesthetically pleasing; they serve the rational mind even as they suggest the dynamics of nature. If there is pure joy in the small decorative universe of the family crests, there is sophistication and elegance when design, function, and material come together, as they do in the Japanese house.

Woven Designs

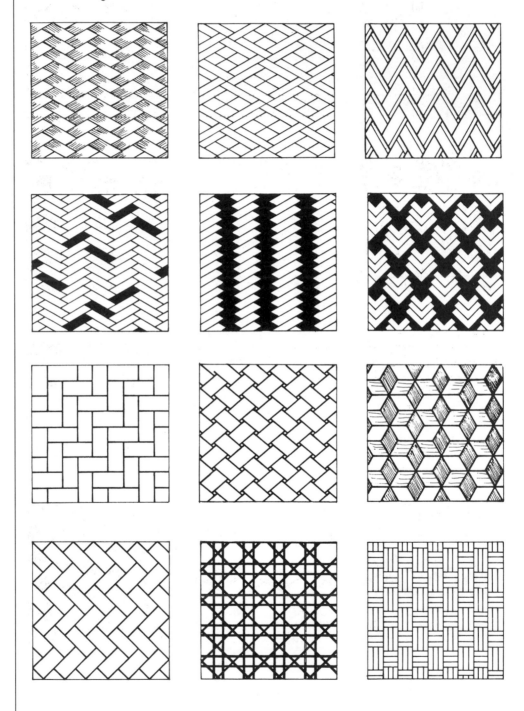

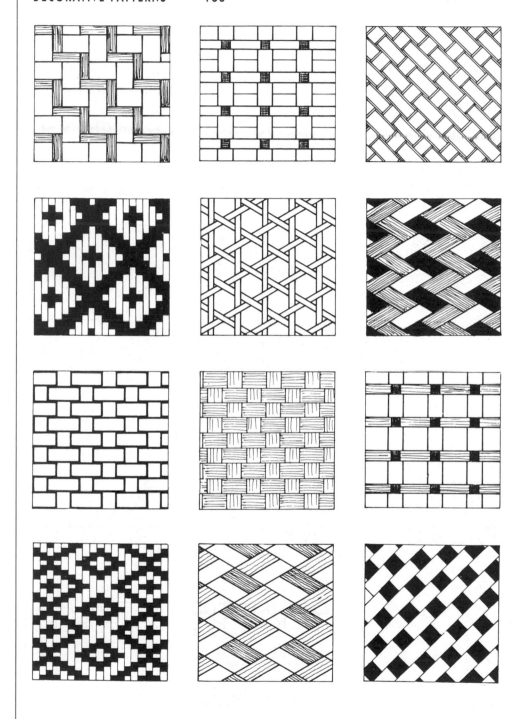

Lattice Designs

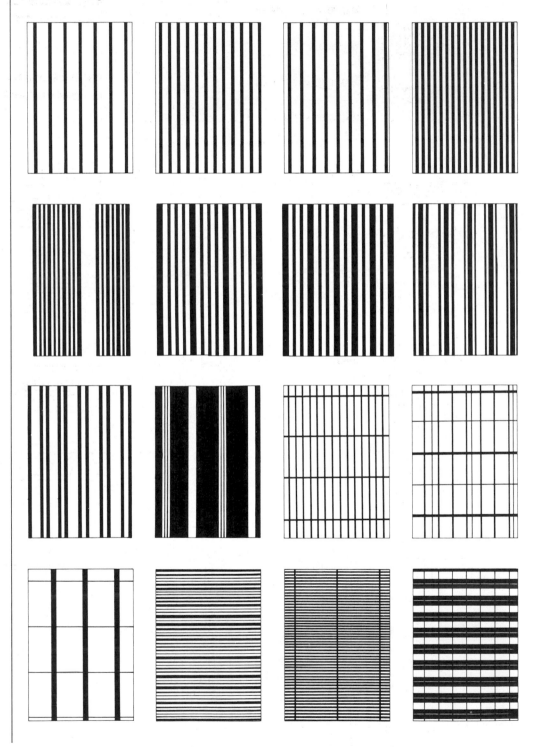

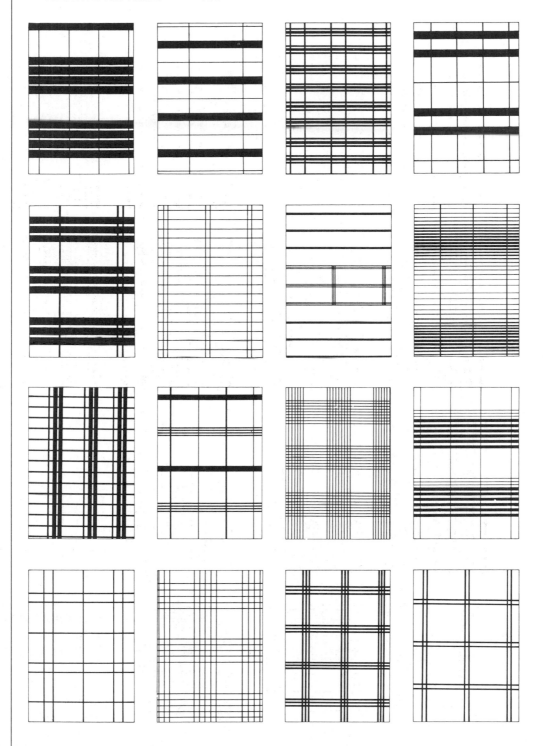

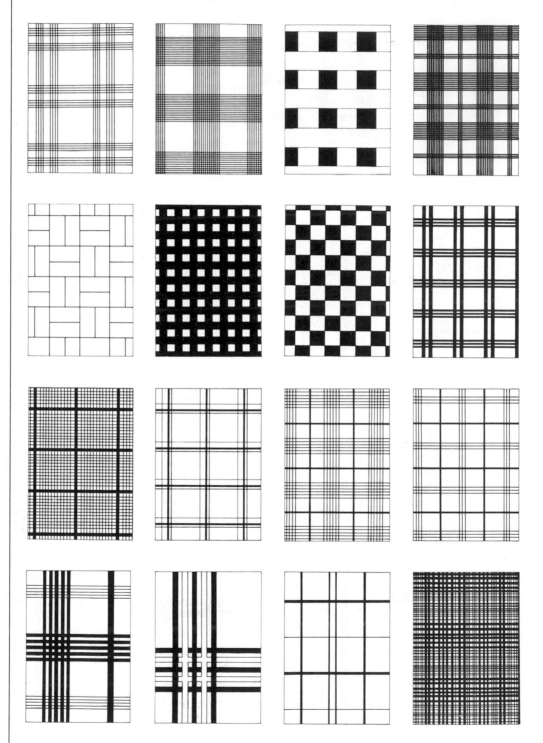

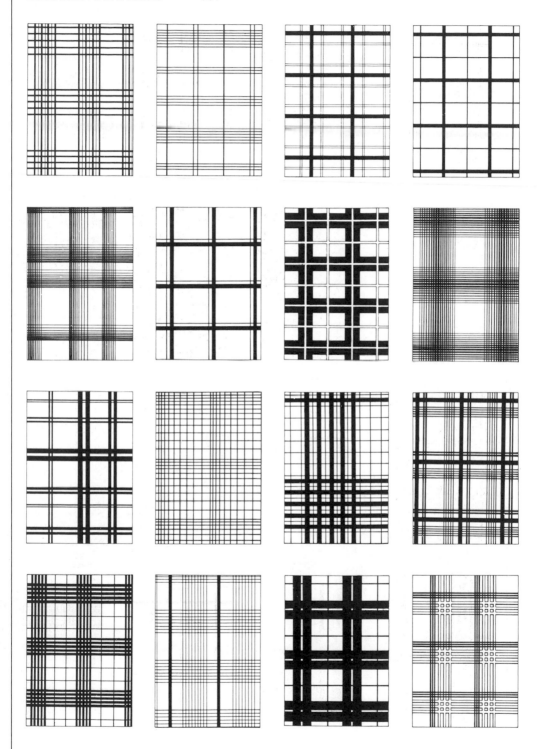

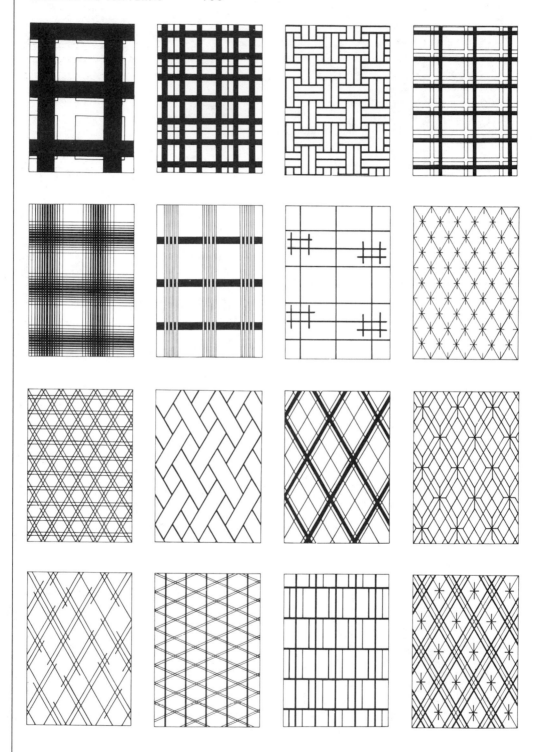

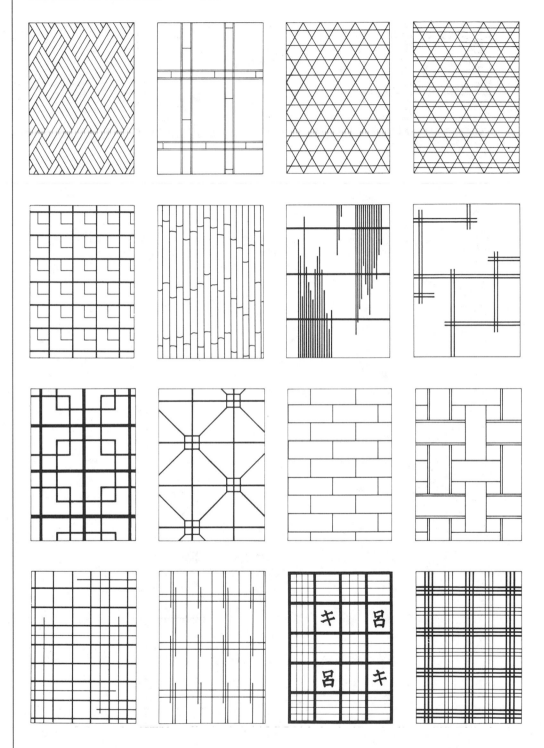

Family Crests (often used on decorative fittings)

 ginkgo

 hemp leaf

 fan

 fan

 rice in circle

 hemp leaf

 fan paper

 folding fans

 rice plant crest

 hermitage

 fan papers

 two fans

 rice sheaf

 ginkgo

 mallow

 two fans

 horse

 plum

 anchor

 well cover

 lobster

 fan

 three anchors

 well cover

 arrowhead

 feathery fan

 plum

 interlocking
well covers

 arrowhead
and stream

 rabbit, moon,
and waves

plum

interlocking
well covers

tortoise

tendrils and
wood sorrel

oak leaf

oak leaf

goose

four-leaf wood
sorrel

mulberry leaf

oak leaf

geese

turnip

wood sorrel

ginkgo

interlocking
squares

tortoise

swords and
wood sorrel

oak leaf

tortoise shell
and flower

paulownia

chrysanthemum

divining marks

tortoise shell
and flower

character
"paulownia"

chrysanthemum
and stream

bamboo hat

tortoise shell
and flower

Chinese
bellflower

chrysanthemum

bamboo hats

pestles

Chinese
bellflower

paulownia

chrysanthemum

hairpin

nail puller

waterwheel

five gourds and
flower

stacked cups

nail pullers

lobed cloud

"Oda" gourds

cherry

top

cross

four gourds
and flower

cherry

chess piece

cut-bamboo
cross

"Genji" wheel

overlapping
circles with
stars

divining marks

bamboo grass
and sparrow

bamboo grass

palm frond

character "city"

bamboo grass
and sparrow

snow on
bamboo grass

sandbar

character
"rice field"

pine, bamboo, plum, and Chinese bellflower

snow on bamboo grass

baby sparrow in snow wheel

Buddhist emblem

cut-bamboo cross

"Yonezawa" bamboo

mallet

plover

hawk feathers

sparrow

butterfly

ivy

single jewel

coin with wave pattern

butterfly

crane

cloves

mandarin orange

shrine gate

origami crane

temple gong

hawk feather

holly leaves

flower in square

sea waves

whirling commas

gourds

flower and swords

encircled pink

whirling commas

two bars

tendrils

noshi ring

whirling
commas

pine-bark
rhombuses

clam

flower

whirling
commas

phoenix

sail in mist

sack

pine-bark
rhombuses

pines

peony

balance weight

three diamonds

pines

three stars

Shinto papered
staff

wisteria

pines

circle of stars

saké pitcher

wisteria

maple leaf

gourds and
flower

Japanese
ginger cloves

pine needles
and bamboo
grass

peach

drawer handle

OTHER DESIGN SOURCES

On the next page is a list of other works that illustrate and describe the design elements shown in this book. Understanding the historical and architectural contexts of the various Japanese design elements will improve your appreciation of them. You will quickly discover that—except for some perfunctory, factory-made shoji—virtually every item you want must be custom made. You will also discover that, in order to accommodate the Japanese elements, your furnishings and your living habits (slamming doors, walking inside with your shoes on) may need to be thoroughly re-examined. How far you take this is up to you, of course. Don't feel you have to restrict yourself to "Japanese" designs. There are many solutions that draw on Japanese architectural principles and also harmonize with Western tastes and furnishings.

Engel, Heinrich. *The Japanese House: A Tradition for Contemporary Architecture*. Tokyo and Rutland, VT: Charles E. Tuttle, 1964. Dense text, but provocative and clearly illustrated.

Hashimoto, Fumio. *Architecture in the Shoin Style: Japanese Feudal Residences.* Trans. H. Mack Horton. Tokyo and New York: Kodansha International, 1981. Historical survey, with an excellent introduction.

Hibi, Sadao. *Japanese Detail: Architecture.* San Francisco: Chronicle Books, 1989. Mainly photographs.

Itoh, Teiji. *The Elegant Japanese House*. Tokyo and New York: Weatherhill, 1969. Beautiful photos. Look for other books by the same author.

Morse, Edward S. *Japanese Homes and Their Surroundings.* Reprint. New York: Dover, 1961. The classic 19th-century study with fine observations.

Nishi, Kazuo, and Kazuo Hozumi. *What Is Japanese Architecture?* Tokyo and New York: Kodansha International, 1983. Excellent overview and drawings.

Rao, Peggy, and Jean Mahoney. *Japanese Accents in Western Interiors.* Tokyo: Shufunotomo, 1988. Household design tips with color photographs.

Slawson, David A. *Secret Teachings in the Art of Japanese Gardens.* Tokyo and New York: Kodansha International, 1987. A wonderful book about Japanese aesthetics and human perception.

Slesin, Suzanne, et al. *Japanese Style*. New York: Clarkson N. Potter, 1987. Lots of photos and ideas.

Ueda, Atsushi. *The Inner Harmony of the Japanese House.* Tokyo and New York: Kodansha International, 1990. Essays about design and living.

van Arsdale, Jay. *Shoji: How To Design, Build, and Install Japanese Screens*. Tokyo and New York: Kodansha International, 1988. Excellent introduction to handtools.

Yagi, Koji. *A Japanese Touch for Your Home.* Tokyo and New York: Kodansha International, 1982. Introduces design elements with many practical tips.